MY HAGAKURE

Paul Askedall

ISBN: 978-0-615-45210-4

This book is dedicated to my loving grandparents,
for I am grateful for having them in times of having nothing,
but even when I am on my feet, they are part of everything
I need.

This is also dedicated to my closest friends,
for you are a rare breed in this world
that I am extremely glad to have found.

Thanks so much for your love and support,
your guidance and great times.

Wow — Interesting & oddly compelling. You touch on things that I have a penchant for — — indeed. You chose your reader wisely.

H.R. for DC Comics

In case of loss, please return to:

Paul E. Askedall, Jr.

████████████████████
████████ ████ ████████

As a reward: $ 200. $\frac{00}{100}$

+ A discussion of
your choice

EA▲

VISITOR

Name: ████████ Tour

Floor/Suite:

Date: 4-10-08

Officer Signature:

Foreword

On a journey, one can experience many a great thing. One can also learn on this journey. No matter where this venture leads, no matter how long it takes, knowledge is an unlimited source. Life is ~~a~~ ~~full~~ full of never-ending choices and an unbelievable amount of possibilities. If you make the right choice you get one step further on the path to your goal, your dream... your destiny. You experience victory, you experience improvement. If you make the wrong choice, the outcome holds a fatal consequence or a minor fault. With the outcome being minor (if fate is willing) you learn from making the wrong decision. You pick yourself up and learn from it. Life is constant and we are constantly learning. One of the greatest experiences in life is to learn something new.

———

✱ Everyday we wake up to a new day of life, work, play. It is like being born again, in our sleep we are at the most innocent, dreaming dreams only we can comprehend on our own. In the hour that we wake we stretch our bodies like a newly-made machine getting into gear. From slumber to stir we continue to move forward, undertaking daily tasks which gather much unwanted stress.

    With all the kinetic negativity, wouldn't you want to get the burdens off your back? Who wouldn't want to wake up without a problem to worry about, without a care in the world? We all wish we can escape the tension of life and just LIVE!

kinetic: adj. 1. relating to the motion of material bodies and the

forces associated therewith;
"kinetic" 2. characterized by motion;
"modern dance has been called
kinetic pantomime" 3. supplying
motive force; "the complex ██████
civilization of which Rome was the
kinetic center" - H.O. Taylor
(syn: energizing, energising)

1. to give energy to; activate or
   invigorate
2. to supply with an electric current

imparting vitality and energy

Kinetic negativity,
negative kinetic energy

Isn't it fascinating how intricately designed the human psyche is, comprised of a zillion thoughts about anything in this world, this universe, or anything in a different dimension? Humans are the most interesting creatures; doing what they do, acting how they do and although they are all part of the same species not one of them is the *exact* same as the other. Identical twins may look alike, dress alike if they choose, even finish each other's sentences— but not every one of their thoughts and feelings are identical. That's how captivating the human soul is. The most natural, unique entity of a spiritual force.

One factor of the human psyche is **emotion**. A changing

consciousness that involves feeling. Being a mental state that is affected subjectively, emotion is a sensitive element— we can be happy all day until something tragic happens or somebody tells us a rumor we weren't expecting. From anger to affection, from happiness to sadness a person cannot choose to feel, only feel through experience.

One of the greatest emotions of human psychology is love. Love is a highly sensitive topic; many people want it and many others have rarely felt it, if at all. This emotion is also a controversial one. When one says to another, "I love you", it can have a few meanings; the first and foremost is important, meaning that person has the strongest like for another coming from the deepest depths of their heart. A statement to be heartbroken. Well, with one exception: if the spouse is disrespectful toward the significant other and/or their friends or family and any kind of abuse is involved. This can be said with families too. If a member of a family disrespects another continuously, they deserve the same treatment. That is a form of karma — in Hinduism and Buddhism, the total effect of a person's actions and conduct during the successive phases of the person's existence, regarded as determining the person's destiny. Karma is the result of a deed or action, being of good or bad consequence depending on the deed. The informal definition of karma is a distinctive aura or feeling.

Referring back to heartbreak,

there goes a gripping and
educational saying:

> 'Tis better to have loved
> and lost than never to
> have loved at all
>
> – Lord Alfred
> Tennyson

It holds true what Tennyson said;
it is better to have loved someone
and be loved, later losing that love,
rather than never having the chance
to love someone or a group of
people and not being loved in
return. That would be horrible,
going through life not being loved
while you look for affection
constantly, only to be turned away
and ignored by others around you,
not having the necessary luxury or
pleasure of having at least one

person love you and take care of you. Everyday going about your business, going to school or to work and continually be surrounded by humans that have the same physical characteristics—two eyes, one nose, one mouth, two arms, two legs—but none are willing to show you the benefit of the doubt of giving you what you hope for everyday, what you pray at least 1 individual will show you – love. The ones around you may show you attention but they don't feel love toward you for some reason. Why? You think you're normal like everyone else so why don't they treat you like everyone else?

Then you go home at the end of the day, there is a hope that maybe a family member will tell you they love you, only to have that hope shattered by a hard, cold shoulder. All you want is to be loved. All you want is to feel special. Growing up, you've been trying your best to find that special someone in your life, someone that you can go to hold and kiss, someone you can confide in and talk to about anything, ANYTHING. You confront every "friend" of the opposite sex and ask them if they'd like to take friendship to the next level, only to find the same answer— "no." Later, after being rejected over and over by the opposite sex, (some more than once) you feel there is no one in this world that will love you and no one will have sympathy for you. Being a loner, you come home just to curl into a ball on your bed and cry... cry because of your pitiful existence, cry because you don't have a significant other to cuddle with, and you keep crying because there's no one to comfort you. So sad.... So you cry yourself to sleep hoping that tomorrow will be better, "there's always tomorrow."

But the next day is no better... you feel yesterday never passed and everything's repetitious. But while still growing up you learn to live with rejection and it's not such a big deal anymore.

Finally, one day you actually run into someone that has feelings for you. After you stopped looking, you actually discover there _is_ somebody that shares more than your feelings for each other, they share a similar childhood. You start dating this amazing person ~~and~~ for one year and six months you both mature as individuals and as a couple and that time you spend with ████████ that special person is the best one year and six months of your life. Then it begins to descend. You seldomly get to see one another and are constantly arguing. There are days you two have that are good and forgiving but then another bad day pops up and that puts more dampening on your relationship. Your spouse starts treating you like shit, even though you've done so much for them, so much... You want to see each other but can't because of financial problems and you lose interest in talking on the phone between the "I love you's" and "I miss you's" because there is nothing to talk about after each silence. You want to see one another, cherish one another, but it becomes more than just a financial problem— your significant other doesn't want to spend the hard-earned money on seeing you for at least one day of the week... sad, isn't it?

Soon you start reverting to your old ways of a depressed loner, minding your own business and again living with a hope that you'll feel that much-wanted and much-needed love once again. Just think of that, you don't want to cheat or leave your precious loved one but you sometimes think of what it would be like with a new spouse... Would it be a better relationship than the one you feel so lonesome in at the moment?.....Or would it be worse?!

As the man of the hour takes his final bow, ask yourself—"Was this a learning experience?" Because if the whole situation (beginning from a lonely and unloved child to a beloved soul mate and travelling full circle) makes you think, if it _at least_ makes you think, do you agree with Alfred Tennyson?

'Tis better to have loved and lost than never to have loved at all...,

∞

✳

There are times I want to stay
home and have fun on my own, rocking
out to music or watching a
kick-ass movie. But when I'm
with friends and we're excited
about something, it feels good.
It feels good being with friends
and doing something fun together,
especially when you have a full
day of freedom.

People should not take friends
or life for granted, no matter
how good or bad your situation
is. As long as you are breathing
there is <u>hope</u>, there is a chance
to turn it all around. Just hope
when you plan something it works,
otherwise it becomes a downer
and you end up asking yourself, "Why?"
or "How?"

✳

Forget what you know, or what you think you know — everything around us is a force of energy. Whether it is good or bad it is still energy and we can connect with it, use it, control it. The greatest forces in this world are Nature and energy from Within (ki, also known as chi or qi) but the general population lacks the discipline and vitality to learn how to become One with their inner chi and the chi of all things. Through years of learning and practicing one can do amazing feats:

- The ability to "feel" somebody behind you
- Have a heightened sense of awareness

- Be quicker than the eye can see

Among other things. Although I

cannot do such acts because I have not yet reached Enlightenment, I am on the path to become One with all things. Today, Wednesday the 17th of May, of the year 2006, I have focused my chi and touched nature without great physical contact.

while I knelt on the grass in my backyard in my usual meditative position, I closed my eyes after aligning my view with the horizon and started a usual breathing pattern, inhale through the nose and exhale through the mouth. After a minute passed, still keeping my eyes closed, I pictured energy flowing through my arms to my hands then through my hands to the ground. I pictured that and concentrated really hard. I ran my hands along the tips of the grass in a semi-circle (see picture 2.) Then, something strange happened: every time I breathed in and ran my hands up the grass, I would breathe out and move my hands down the grass but every time I breathed out and moved my hands down, there would appear a breeze. The breeze was slight at first but gradually increased. Astonished that I was actually doing this, I broke concentration and the wind settled. I opened my eyes, inhaled then exhaled and felt one more small gust of wind then it died.

'Tis possible to do great things with one's chi, all that needs to be done is focus and practice. Take the Wachowski brothers' blockbuster hit The Matrix for example. Morpheus tells Neo he is as fast as he wants to be. He tells Neo, "Don't *think* you are, *know* you are." You know that phrase Mind over Matter? The mind is a miraculous thing. If you <u>believe</u> you can, not think but believe you can, you can accomplish stunts you never thought you could do.

Afterthought: I was aware what was happening but when I focused on it, made the action become part of my thoughts, the wind stopped. With meditation, if something happens out of the ordinary you should be aware of the action but don't allow it to become part of your thought process. Don't <u>think</u> about it. Keep your mind empty and just know it's happening.

☺ ...... ☹

Everyone deserves to be happy

<u>Happy</u>

"All I want in life is to be happy."

The girl in my dreams was whence forethought, now I am full circle she shall be forgot

2 years

Some days when I am bombarded with life's negativity I feel like packing a bag and just leaving. I want to get away, go some place better. Sometimes I feel this isn't the life for me.

One day when I'm ready..... I will leave.

I am close to what I want to do, my childhood dream...so damn close.... I can grasp it but I won't be able to touch it yet. As for <u>where</u> I want to be, that is a place I yearn to be in my life, a place where I so desperately want to live........ but that 'place' is farther than my 'job', my career.... <u>Think</u> ahead and <u>plan</u> ahead but <u>live</u> one day at a time.

An old quote: "Don't let the bastards bring you down."

Positive thinking can get you far, just don't assume. Assumptions are for the minds of the foolhardy, expect an unexpected outcome and you will not be caught by surprise. Scouts said it best. Their motto: "Always be prepared"

If the world was thrown into an ice age or a massive heat wave, I would rather experience another ice age because the darkness can't kill your skin! Then there are the factors of clothing; with extreme cold you can ~~wear~~ wear multiple layers of clothing and other accessories like goggles, caps, and gloves. There's only so much you can take off in the heat before being publicly indecent, unless you're in your own home. Then comes food. Most food, canned or otherwise, can stand being in the cold as it can be heated to be comfortably edible. Fruits can also bear the cold better than the heat, for the high temperatures can make the fruit moldy and gather bacteria. The freezing cold can either slow the growth of bacteria or can stop it completely, therefore preserving the food. But there're drawbacks; like the heat melting things, short-circuiting electronics and starting fires, the subzero temperatures can freeze, Freeze, FREEZE. Frozen electronics, frostbite, dead animals and people. An ice age I would be able to handle longer than a massive heat wave.

* I like cold, dark climates *

Random fact: Mosquitos are more attracted to you after eating a banana.

Random fact: The youngest girl to give birth was a 5 year old Peruvian girl

* Snopes.com

As male and female mature, they constantly look in the mirror to check themselves of imperfections. Girls/women more than boys/men unless the male is infatuated with himself!

They check themselves in the mirror to make sure their hair is perfect or there's nothing in their teeth or other qualities   stand out that would embarrass them or make them uncomfortable. They check themselves to look good for peers or for that one drop-dead sexy stranger they hope to capture the attention of. Guys will flex their muscles and girls will adjust their bras or shirt to give the impression of a big cup size or to show cleavage. Both sexes will give a quick huff into a cupped hand to inspect their breath.

Since humans are pack animals, they need to be part of a crowd, mingling and being in contact with others of their kind. By "others of their kind" I don't mean in racial terms, I mean the same species — "homo sapien."

People of all races, genders (there are more than 2 if you count she-males) and ages have to be included into society to stay sane and healthy. They try to become part of a niche, or more truly, find their niche in society. We all want to have an audience to discuss issues or ideas with or to have someone we can go to for consolatory support or even guidance. There are others that will even go so far as to choose an aggressor to argue with or to, just to vent their anger/thoughts/problems or to fulfill their delusion of being superior and arguing their point. As a general whole, people want to be liked. They want gratification for doing a good deed or upon getting a favor done. For example, if a friend of mine asked me to do a big favor for them, something they need done with utmost importance, and I do that favor (and I get it done right away or accomplish the task very well), I expect that friend to thank me, to acknowledge the fact that I did them that favor. If they don't thank me I at least hope my friend is considerate of me later on. A person's gratification is not demanded (although to some it is) but we like to hear it. Gratification gives us pride and for some it raises self-confidence. A confidence that not only encourages ourselves we are capable of doing a good deed but a confidence that we're a good person.

└ Many individuals need or want that kind of confidence.

After finding a niche, people become comfortable in themselves. They may not be aware of it but they create a comfort zone full of security and belonging. Once a person is taken out of their comfort zone, living can become difficult and that person can deal with the situation in one of two ways: try to revert back to living in that comfort zone and not take on any challenges, OR— move forward and build another comfort zone around the new and challenging part of life.

Back to talking with peers and discussing topics, it is a great right to have freedom of speech and freedom of expression. Nobody likes being controlled and having the ability to express one's views and opinions, and talk openly and gain insight and critiques or criticism on anything is important in a consumer- and community-driven nation. Critiques and criticism are substantial factors in improvement but a numerous amount of people dislike criticism, let alone take it. Those individuals are either on a power trip and find importance in their arrogance or they're close-minded (or both). You can't be close-minded in the world today, there are just too many good things (or bad things, depending on how you look at it) which include music, film, literature, and clothing among other subjects of social design including cooking, art and architecture. Plus, if you're not open-minded you're not living life to the fullest! You are not allowing creativity to flow through your mind. Sure there are a handful of stubbornly unreceptive blokes that will SAY they're not narrow-minded... but when it comes to discussing topics that concern certain likenesses of the other person(s), they'll be quick to state that they "don't like that" or "don't focus on that".... THEN HOW

ARE YOU NOT OBSTINATE!? (firmly or stubbornly adhering to one's purpose, opinion, etc. Also: characterized by inflexible persistence or an unyielding attitude)

Open Your Mind!

FREE YOUR MIND.

Everybody has a right to be biased because of how they think or what they think, no matter how small or stupid or outrageous, it's their opinion, but sometimes a person's view can be too radical or asinine and that's when we tell them to get an education.

'Tis also funny when somebody starts an argument with you between opposing viewpoints and you discover you have a higher intellect and/or education than them but that person is still trying to sound smarter than you... Ha ha you are less experienced in the ways of discussion, yet you try and be smarter?

Do not embarrass yourself puny human, quit now while you are still behind! Tuck your tail inbetween your legs and go sit in the corner!!!

* I don't think people should be judged by their age, but their intelligence.

I have friends who are exceptionally younger than me that are well-knowledgeable in ethics and culture and are fully aware of societal shortcomings. On top of that those same friends are maturer than a few older friends of mine as well as a huge number of childish adults among the masses.

*RANDOM fact: Some older model cordless phones call 911 by themselves when their batteries are dying.

I had an interesting thought: I indulged an energy drink, a Monster (one of my faves), and I had to go to the restroom within twenty-some odd minutes. I know I have a fast metabolism so ~~as~~ ~~⊛~~ as I relieved myself I pictured the energy drink sliding down my throat, dropping off all the B-Vitamins and Ginseng and Caffeine along the way, depositing all its contents and sugar throughout my body and then immediately leaving my system as water. Tis like a speeding train with all its passengers jumping off at random stations and then still going. I feel the Monster working too, making my body warm and jumpy, like I want to get up and shout and jump around and get the acquired energy out. The drink passed through my body, deposited its nutritional contents, then upon finishing its job, is released as an empty train, a liquid that is now void of its canned ingredients. If you want to get scientific, its a liquid returning to its natural state; a water that is combined with juice and other doses of minerals and then distributed, thus turning it back into water. Or a variant of water... the bodily 'lemonade'. Heh heh.

oxymoron: Temporarily blinded for life

Riddle: A man hung himself in a room. His friend found him and there was nothing under him but a puddle of water. How did he do it?
... I found this fun

If I were a....

Animal: Cheetah to know how it feels to run 70-77 miles per hour, Bat to experience flight and navigate with sonar, Armadillo to feel how it is to have natural armor

Planet: Jupiter, to experience having such large mass and have anticyclonic storms that are the size of Earth(roughly) and that can last from 177 years to 340 or more, and have such strange cloud motion of the hot gases that comprise the atmosphere. For instance, eddies (the swirling of a fluid and the reverse current created when the fluid flows past an obstacle. The moving fluid creates a space devoid of downstream-flowing water on the downstream side of the object. Fluid behind the obstacle flows into the void creating a swirl of fluid on each edge of the obstacle, followed by a short reverse flow of fluid behind the obstacle flowing up-stream, toward the back of the obstacle form and Converge. Also called eddy fords, they are part of fluid dynamics. A Coriolis force forms and forces cooler air to fall back into a swirling motion that can be many kilometers in diameter.

A <u>Coriolis</u> <u>effect</u> is a funny (peculiar) happening. If a person was on a rotating frame of reference observing an object, and the object was on a straight path, the object would seem to be on a curved path.

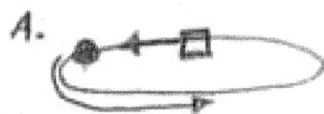
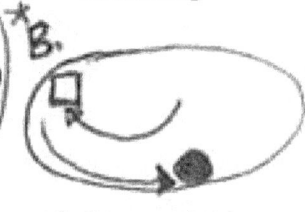

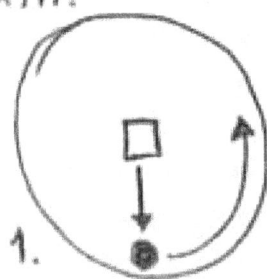

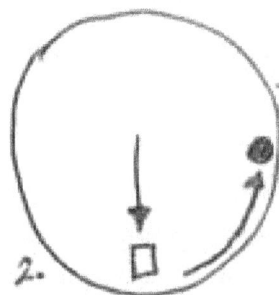

● = observer
□ = object

*Coriolis effect

* wikipedia.org as my source

<u>Integrated computer part</u>: Graphics card, because I wouldn't care how I looked or how small I was as long as I got the job done beautifully and attracted people to the result. Am I giving a clue, hinting to some part of my personality, a characteristic of my lifestyle?....perhaps. 😏

I'm not superficial, unlike a large sum of people in this world. To me looks aren't everything when it comes to liking someone, or in other ▓▓▓ instances, having a good car. Most people will immediately judge a stranger based upon their physical appearance. Men will judge women by their breast size, their butts, and whether or not the women are skinny. Girls will judge guys by how muscular they are, their butts or even the size of their hands(don't ask why). A person's face is a neutral physicality, seeing as some people won't mind having a mate who has a great body but (to others) lacks a model-status face, and vice versa with a mate that has an amazingly attractive face but needs improvement in the body region. Really, being attracted to someone is based on a person's own taste... the thing is, too many people have a taste for the same things. Granted, living in a nation where scantily-clad females are all over the television screen and with industries that use sex and sexual appeal and intimidation to attract people to buy their products, one can expect the general public to want nothing less than the hottest spouse in the world. Growing up and being surrounded by the most alluring physicalities can have someone become superficial, but I guess that also depends on how the person lives, what he/she likes and dislikes. It's just being surrounded by hot models in almost every form of promotional advertising can leave a person open to liking only people that are as hot as the models that are shown to us.

There are 3 categories of indulgence:

LIKE   WANT   NEED

People are attracted to what they like and so they will try and find what they want based on their likes, but what they like and want can be different from what they need. Although what people need can also include factors of what they like and want.

Random
Fact: If human brain cells were people, there'd be enough of them to populate 25 planets like ours

⊕ Dr. Rudolf Flesch is a renowned authority on language and says that he worked for almost 20 years before fully realizing the connection between thoughts, speech, and writing.

—Thinking is silent speech, and speech is simply thinking out loud.— After the action of speaking, communication can be taken a step further.

—Writing is a way of speaking on paper—

Dr. Flesch is one of the many expert communicators mentioned in Donald Walton's book, Are You Communicating?

'Tis an extremely educational guidebook I believe EVERYONE should read! Not only does it educate a person in becoming an interesting conversationalist, it improves their use in business ethics and language overall.

I don't like when people make decisions <u>for</u> me... that is a type of control and nobody likes being controlled. At least TELL me or ask me before the decision is made.

ꝺ

There is a line between patience and tolerance, even though it's a thin line, it's still there, it still borders on both characteristics.

In a way I wish there were more minutes in an hour, more hours in a day, more days in a week, more weeks in a month, and more months in a year. Time flies not only when you're having fun but also as you grow older... because as one accumulates years of age and experience (hopefully), they take on more and more responsibility(s). Unless you're a dependent sapling that continually whines when asked by their parent or guardian to move out and ends up being a 50 year old still living in mommy's or daddy's house because you didn't want to accept responsibility when it knocked on your door. *Whew*

So the more responsibilities you have and the busier you are, the more you have a set schedule and have to do things by a certain time. When I was a little kid, I woke up in the morning and played computer games for hours on end. Then I would play make-believe with my younger brother and sister or go outside and ride a bike, play in the dirt and just be merry... and it seemed like forever, although forever would be cut short when it was dinner time! Even in school as a young lad time was slow when I wanted it to go fast (that's also because I was thinking of it and it wouldn't happen... that's something I learned in elementary school — if you WANT time to go faster, it's not going to happen!) until I went to lunch or a free period and wanted time to go slow 'cuz I was havin' so much fun, no sooner than I thought it, the bell would ring... curse you Father Time!!! hee hee. In the Western world time can be measured down to a second and in Western theory time is viewed as a straight line, a single, continuous path. Referring to time viewed by Eastern philosophy, it is a circle. With every single thing living or inanimate, there is a beginning, middle, end, then rebirth. Plants are planted, grown, destroyed and then replanted. Babies are born. They grow. People live their lives. They die. Their souls live on in another plane of existence. Eastern cultures don't measure life as minutes, hours, etc. They measure life through seasons and other natural cycles. Maybe if westerners measured time the same way, people wouldn't worry about how old they are or how long they have on a project... unless the ~~plans~~ project needs to be completed before the sun is "high in the sky" tomorrow. Since we wouldn't have calendars or clocks, it would feel like we would be living longer lives. No regard to precise measurements of time we would live our lives within the seasons of nature.

I think it would be a lot less stressful...... at least for people that don't already meditate.

★ In business the Japanese have time gaps called "mah," and in those time gaps businessmen use the time to meet and discuss issues and view the current situation before making a decision for the company or negotiating with other companies. They also use the time to meditate and even sleep. The mah periods are resting sessions in other words.

American businesses should adopt that strategy, or at least give it a try. It probably wouldn't last too long knowing "time is money" to many and running around being stressed is part of the job. There's no time for corporations to take a temporary break to relax, think, and talk to others about the future of the company upon making a certain decision. Given, companies do have meetings to discuss decision making and the like but with the tension built up because of deadlines and pressure from executives, it would be nice to relieve at least some of that stress... unless there is no resting period in the adopted, Americanized version of mah Western corporations would probably deem the resting part of the time gaps unnecessary or even stupid by some businessmen's standards. Who knows? I could be wrong and it might help Western business instead of hinder them. Personally I think mah periods would be a helpful cycle.

———

When I went to Seattle, Washington and waited to be picked up by the loading/unloading dock, I looked across the street and saw the airport parking garage. 'Twas a cool ~~sight~~ sight to behold; the whole parking garage looked like an enormous bunker. Whether it could be a building from the Dune series or an alien structure, it did not look like it belonged there (or here, on earth). I enjoy ~~~~ unique architecture!

Fact finally known: Elvis Presley was naturally born blonde.

We live our lives knowing what we've been taught and the experiences we go through. Once we are told some random fact or useful information that we can apply to our daily lives or at least spread word to everybody else, we feel better knowing that information (or at least I do).
Speaking about spreading word, I feel sharing philosophical quotes and phrases with people is an enlightening deed and can allow others to view life differently and even feel happier about their new outlook. I understand there are a bunch of quotes that are pseudo-wise and have absolutely no philosophical meaning and

are created to sound wise, but I stray from those certain sayings. The sayings I write down to remember and pass on are strictly educational and life-changing.

When I start discussing fortune cookies you'll probably laugh and joke about living by quotes coming from a randomly-inserted strip of paper hidden within a Chinese food take-home snack. I don't take every single fortune to heart but the fortunes I do collect/keep always end up being incorporated into my life somehow.

One fortune I kept was:

"Drastic means aren't always necessary"

Having a debt and not being able to save any money, and working a job that doesn't pay me enough comfortably to pay off my debt and buy food for myself, I was aggravated and saddered. I felt like finding a better job to extinguish my debt faster and start saving. The job I have as a librarian doesn't pay well but I can check my email, work on school projects or personal projects, and help students with computer issues. My job is very lenient and convenient. Everyday at school (working) I come closer to finishing stuff I've been working on for awhile. ~~So~~ So thinking of that quote I took from the fortune cookie, maybe I shouldn't take drastic measures and get a new job right away. During my free time at school I can draw and improve my talent so when the time comes and I graduate, from here I can find a career and the talent I have will be good enough to be hired.

Besides "drastic means aren't always necessary," another saying I live by is, "The longer the wait, the more worth it it'll be." And <u>that</u> quote has come up in my life as well.

☆

–"Never tell your problems to anyone,
20% don't care and the other 80%
are glad you have them."–

"There are 3 types of people in
this world: those who make things
happen, those who watch things
happen, and those who wonder what
happened."

↑   ↑

I didn't write these

Nor this

↓

"I have not failed. I've just found
10,000 ways that won't work."

–Thomas
Alva
Edison

These sayings, among the hundreds I
have recorded, have inspirational and
philosophical value and have helped me
approach life's difficulties easier.

After watching the big screen adaptation of Chuck Palahniuk's novel Fight Club (years ago), and later reading the book, I realized that the message Tyler Durden was expressing was the firm clarity people should be educated in; that society today is the middle man of history and that we have a false understanding of who we are. So, upon praising the book and film, and creating a fight club with a group of friends, I created a brutally honest introduction to Fight Club:

What is Fight Club, you ask? Fight Club is a release. A release from life, a release from the ever-hoping image that you'll be big and famous in life. That image is a continuous message that mocks you in your sleep, when you wake, when you eat, when you shit, when you fuck, and when you work. Fight Club is a big slap in the face, a kick in the stomach, it is a knee to the groin, yelling at you, telling you to "WAKE UP!" because you will not become an idol; but Fight Club will make you see yourself as an icon, a somebody, anybody! Anybody else than the boring, self-pitied dog that you are everyday. How can you know yourself if you've never been in a fight? Fight Club will teach you what you're capable of, it will shape you into a man. The man you become will look back on the man you once were and despise him. Despise him for being a naive nobody, doing nothing in life.

This is your life. Do something.

My YouTube channel is a full spectrum of my mind and interests. I am a soldier, a poet, a rocker, a relaxer, a student, a teacher, a vampire, a friend, an enemy, a punk, a hunter, a model, an actor. I am silly and random, practical and precise, full of virtue and toning down my vice. I have an open mind and accept challenges. Why? Because the more effort and determination you put into a project, the more it pays off in the end. Plus overcoming obstacles help build the person you become and the future you strive for. Effort isn't effort if it doesn't hurt.

I've been through much in my life, I'm sure everyone has in a point or so in their lives, and that's why my channel, "No Bounds", is a display of colors from a full spectrum.

Sunday August 5, 2007

I spent the weekend out on the north shore of long island with a friend and her husband. Her husband drove me around to show me the community; very pristine environment it is. The general area is an independent residence, I looked around and saw shops and other businesses that were family-owned. There are no big-time, corporate companies to be found; the only one I saw is a single CVS drugstore. It's good to see places that don't sell out to a main-stream business, or ~~that~~ that aren't forced to change or give it up.

My only difference of opinion is the personality of the wealthy residents. My friend's husband was telling me many of the people have a "higher-than-thou" mindset. Just because you have the money to afford expensive items most people only dream of buying, doesn't mean you should treat others like trash who aren't so fortunate. Yes, okay, you've gotten this far in life and accumulated enough money to retire and sip whine and eat cheese in your beach-side hut, you may think that gives you the right to think highly of yourself and see yourself above all others and live the rest of your life like a king...., but then you become an asshole in that mindset. And we all know the world hates assholes! !!

Most of them were either born into wealth or acquired it through little hardships. I mean, I feel I'm meant for something greater in life but when I do become rich or at least earn a nice amount, I'm not going to look at poor or middle class citizens as inferior! I came from that life. I'm struggling to reach the top and I look at myself as just another human being (or vampire), without an ego and just someone who ▓▓▓ wants to be happy in life and who wants his friends and family to be happy.

That is part of the philosophy of the martial arts. Humility.   This doesn't mean to be completely passive and let everyone walk all over you, it means to portray yourself as you truly are: an everyday person trying to live life. No matter what you do, do it without arrogance and do not live with an ego. Even if someone taunts you for one reason or another, let them humiliate you with words. They are not important unless they try and physically hurt you or your loved ones.
To live in humility   is to live without egos, and to live without egos is

to live in humility.

"A bend in the road is not the end of the road, unless you fail to make the turn."

Life's challenges and obstacles are only temporary, although challenges can be obstacles and obstacles can be challenging. So buckle up, 'cause it's all part of the ride.

Some days when I find solace, when I am content in that moment in time, I can't help but smile because I am happy...

"Happiness is not something ready made. It comes from your own actions."

Two topics I will not discuss in this book: Politics and Religion. Of course I have my own views and opinions, but politics and religion are the two most sensitive subjects in the world. Religion even more so than politics, in my eyes. Wars are waged over religion, yet religion is supposed to represent peace. Politicians are running a nation for its people, yet they make decisions that drive against the rights or liberties of the very people they're in power for..... that is all I will express.

"There are only two mistakes one can make along the road to truth; not going all the way and not starting."   — Buddha

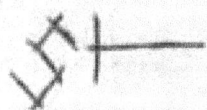

Many people use an alarm clock
to wake up their sleepy heads, or
they use their cell phone and set
it to play a merry melody or a
loud noise at the time they need.
I use my body. My mind is a
natural alarm clock; when I need
or want to be up at a certain time,
I just think of the time and it's
programmed into my head. When I
wake, I glance at the clock and
it'll be the exact time I wanted, or
a few minutes before.

You can probably say it's because
my body recognizes the 24 hour
schedule in my life, but I can break
away from my daily sleeping routine any
day, any time and take naps or sleep
longer or shorter than usual and my
mind won't fail me. That is, of course,

unless I die in my sleep....

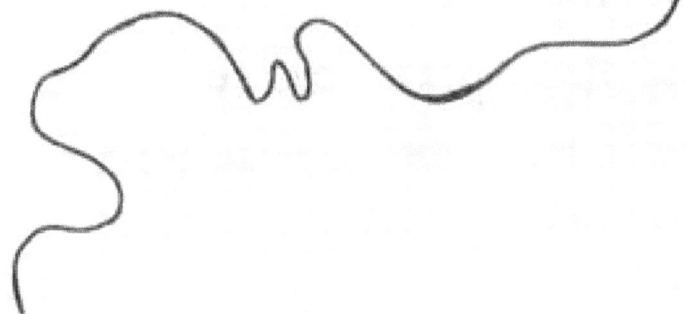

While we're on the subject of sleep, I would like to share my experiences of slumber.

There are times when I wake up and, if I had a dream, I would record it into my Dream Journal. Other times I would wake and think to myself, "That was weeeiirrd!" and wouldn't be able to put it into words because it was such a strange dream, it would have to be experienced to know how extraordinarily bizarre the dream was. For those of us that dream, there are episodes of a good or bad mind trip but some of the bad mind trips I experience are still enjoyable. Since there are genres of literary presentation labeled fiction and science fiction, and even non-fiction that is based on facts and reality — I created a new genre called "dreamfiction" or "cloudfiction" that consists of recorded events within the reality of our minds during a dream state.

Dreams can feel extremely real. So real in fact, I will wake up and think (upon remembering the dream) that what transpired actually happened. There are also times where, in a dream, I'll put money in my pocket and upon waking I reach down to take out the money from my pocket (which in fact are nonexistent since my pj's don't have pockets) and pull out air. "Damn," I think to myself. :(

Twas like instinct to reach down and check how much I took and if it returned with me from my dream state to the real world. Dreams are a strange and amazing thing. I have created a dream journal and have recorded events of my unconscious experiences, something I like to call dreamfiction. Dreams are a miraculous thing; at times they can be wild, random, and misinterpreting. Other times they can be focused and in a constant flow, like life is constantly flowing. It's the thought of experiencing a world inside your head, a world and people that your unconscious creates. It's really fascinating how, awake, our minds (to the naked eye) are not moving, and outside it in the physical world we move and talk and are mobile and we can travel anywhere on this globe, full of billions of different people of all ages and ethnicities, full of towering buildings that touch the sky above us... while during sleep it is the reverse where our bodies are not moving but there is so much going on in our minds, so much moving inside, and in a world similar to that of reality but at the same time NOT too similar.

My psychology professor once told the class not to use the word 'subconscious' because it's a Hollywood term and is not a true term in the study of psychology. I dare to differ! First, I understand the term is avoided in academic settings and it's defined in the Concise Oxford Dictionary in terms similar to the unconscious layer of the mind. Subconscious may also be described as the preconscious, or information contained in the mind and can be recalled by thinking of it... but that would still be part of the conscious mind. I learned in the same professor's class that any thought, person/place/thing, or word that we can recall or dwell on, ANYTHING we can think about while we are awake is part of the conscious, whereas the unconscious is the dark place in our mind (filled with the most disgustingly gritty and horrid thoughts that you can't even imagine) that we are not able to delve into from our conscious thought process. Since we have layers of our mind (conscious being the outer and unconscious being the bottom/inner layer) the term subconscious should be the boundary between the two states of mind should it not? The transition from sleep to awake? ... I asked my professor what he would call that state of mind if not 'sub'conscious — he told me a dream state. While it _is_ a dream state, if people can interact with others outside of sleep or just a moment or two before they wake up, that has to be another state, another layer of consciousness. Beneath the conscious mind but above the unconscious. Yes,

actions and speech/words that take place during a period of sleep can be referred to as "sleep-walking" and "sleep-talking", so let me pinpoint the ~~subconscious~~ subconscious into a precise and structured understanding: not the actions or words while sleeping, but the state of mind ONLY <u>emerging</u> <u>from</u> <u>sleep</u>. Also, the subconscious is only experienced in a dream state. It borders on sleep and awake, and connects reality to our mind's reality. For example, a friend of mine told me just before he woke up one day, he was dreaming about someone and ~~that~~ someone was calling his name ~~over~~ over and over, so he hit them. A moment later he woke up and that friend was standing by him, asking why my friend hit them. That friend of his was calling his name to wake him up. Another account similar to this was when I was late

to get up for school and I was
dreaming. In my dream I kept hearing
my name being called and when I awoke
I discovered my grandmother and my
dad were both trying to get me up,
banging on my bedroom door. I heard
them in my dream, or in my sleep, just
like my friend Chuck heard his name
in his dream. In some instances, like
with people suffering from insomnia,
the mind plays tricks on you because
you are so exhausted and can hallucinate.
You may interact with people that aren't
there or real, or you can hear voices
and you no longer can distinguish what's
real and what's not. Now you're probably
thinking, "What does that have to do with
dreams and states of mind?" Well, it can
relate to life feeling like a dream or the
condition of not knowing the difference
between reality and the dream world. But
I am straying off the path of discussion

I shall return to the main topic.

Another great happening is when I need/want to wake up from a bad dream or I have the consciousness to know I need to be up, I simply close my eyes in my dream and think to myself, "Wake up, I need to wake up," and I open my eyes in bed, awake for a certain time or awake to escape certain doom. Some nightmares it takes me 2 or 3 tries before I awake. But yeah, that's how I leave my dream world, my unconscious state: close my eyes in my dream, think of waking up, and I open my real eyes. That's my gateway, the "passing through the threshold." There are times when I wake up around, let's say, 5:30 am. I have to be up at 6:45 am. I'll close my eyes and go back to sleep. If I don't dream, I can wake up and get out of bed at

6:45 or a little before. If I DO
dream and I'm walking around some-
place or talking to someone in my
mind's reality, I tend to overshoot
that time and I end up waking late.
It has happened countless times
before. I know when you dream you're
in a deep sleep and it takes your
brain more energy to bring you out
of slumber, it pushes your body to get
moving. So to sum it up, if I dream
I wake up later than planned. If I
don't dream I wake up right on time.

Now I will close this discussion so
I take a nap and you take a break...
and I write later. Be gone with
you!

Random toot: Poor leg circulation
(Peripheral Artery Disease or P.A.D.)
is a dangerous condition and can
lead to heart attack or stroke.

———

September 19, 2007
Wednesday

This morning I awoke at 6:11
to stretch and meditate before
breakfast. I was in my backyard
and while having my mind empty, I
took in the fresh air and listened to
nature; the morning birds chirping and
singing, crickets still stridulating....
it was peaceful. Serene.
It's good to get up early in the
morning to get things done and have
the rest of the day off, or at least
work on more things that you've been

putting off and haven't had the necessary time to work with. Start a new day in life by getting up at the ass-crack of dawn; even if you're not an early bird and despise mornings, take a day or two or three each month and get started bright 'n' early. If you get tired in the middle of the day, take a nap! No biggie. I know there's the quota of 'getting enough sleep' and that's important for your health but just do it. At least once. Come on. Be a victim to peer pressure *poke, poke* Just kidding... but wake up at least one morning at either five, six, or seven o'clock and take in the new day.

When you do wake that early, and you breath in the clean, cool air and listen to the beautiful stillness, you realize it's literally a <u>new</u> day; the air isn't thick with pollution and isn't recycled from everybody breathing it.

the lawn cats Shit nothing This sucks Yes! To
Crap. I can't forget to pay that bill! This is
up there There's He's not going anywhere.
Ha!
What are you looking at? 6,000 poun
ish them a happy birthday funny
$18 \times 35 = ?$ Oh yeah What What would happ
Dammit AWW... No, don't do
It's green! Let's go!
That politician doesn't know what he's ta
to see that movie that close...
Only 4? Pshhh... pancake batt
C'mon, c'mon, c'mon carrots

This is an unfocused, untrained mind full of thoughts and worries.

Meditation helps.

This is an empty, trained mind,
open to any given situation and free
to concentrate on a single thought.

Ha, I just saw a commercial for Veramyst. While the brief ad ~~was~~ was going on, I spotted at the bottom "The way Veramyst works is still mis-understood." That's great... it's a marketed medicine, yet the ones that created it don't fully understand its process of working. Oh well. As long as it works and/or makes money right?

"Virtue is persecuted more by the wicked man than it is loved by the good."

My friend Chris' cats have personalities. One is a partially blind female
that is old and only allows Chris and
his family to pick her up or even pet
her. The second is a retired warrior,
a male who, in his younger years, brought
home dead birds and mice as trophies.
When someone not of Chris' family
comes over, he meows and whines until
he finds the stranger non-threatening.
He also likes Death Metal; when Chris
blasts Death Metal in his room, the
Warrior enters and sits on Chris'
bed to enjoy it. After Chris plays
a little Power Metal/Epic Metal, he'll
leave the room and in will come
Smokey because he likes Power/Epic
Metal. I find it funny. Smokey's
his third feline and the youngest one.

he's also the furriest/fluffiest.

My ferrets have personalities as well. The boy in the duo, Winston, is a smart one. If he wants to come out of the cage and I'm not releasing him, he'll get on the 2nd floor platform and lay on his tummy with his head on his paws and look adorable. Like so:

It's like he's saying, "I'm cute, you know you wanna let me out!"

So I give in to the cuteness and let him run around my room, or in the backyard if I'm not too busy. Also, when he's running around and I pick him up, Winston licks my hand or arm to either tell me he loves me or to try and be cute again so I can put

him down and not back in his room.
(I look at my ferrets as more than
just pets, they're part of my family.
And my best friends. That's most
likely how everyone sees their pet,
as family. Unless you no longer want to
have the responsibility of taking care
of it and you leave the animal in some
dumpster or in a bag in the back of
a store.)

All aminals have a personality, they
each have a soul. You may not notice
it, it can be one tiny habit or
characteristic that is different from
another animal of the same species.
   One benefactor of an animal having
a distinct personality or behavior is
the environment it grew up in and/or
how it was treated. Of course it wouldn't
be a 'benefitting' factor if the poor

creature was subjected to abuse and neglect (which is another form of abuse but anyway...)

SÁVE THE CRITTERS!

* And yes I spelled animal wrong. On purpose. I think the word aminal is different and darling !! :)

The Tunguska meteorite that struck Siberia in 1908 was the most shocking explosion in Earth's history.

An asteroid falling to Earth is a meteor and when it hits the ground it's called a meteorite

A few theories of the horrific and mysterious explosion is a meteor, UFO, or a comet. The trees in the Tunguska swamp contained Carbon(C) which is also rich in comets, but some physicists debate the Tunguska explosion to be caused by a comet. Russian scientists are still trying to prove it was a comet. American scientists are saying it was an asteroid. Recently, scientists and physicists are saying it ~~was~~ ~~could~~ caused by a subterranean volcano, but there is no trace of magma. Until the truth is finally revealed/uncovered, there will be many theories that will be brought to light and they will all be speculative.

One phenomenon caused be the Tunguska event called "Bright Night" is when the night sky is so bright it seems that night is day... hence the name, Bright Night.

▷CORRUPTION

   I saw a story on the news about a worker (or 2?) getting badly beaten by two Yankees fans just because they were Red Sox fans. Getting on the subject of sports, I find it absurd how far people take winning and losing, even if they're not playing! It's a game. You're watching it, not playing. Plus, unless you're investing in team stocks or betting thousands of dollars on a win, I see NO reason to get up in arms about losing. Or on the whole topic of sports altogether. A friend I used to work with at Modell's Sporting Goods told me when he traveled to Boston, there was unofficial Red Sox merchandise that read, "Jeter Sux It." How "sucks" is spelled is unknown to me but they mean the same thing. I thought wow, that's a bit brash! It's pretty immature how people react to losing or just toward another team.

Referring back to the newsflash, the attorney for the two suspects told reporters, "The two men did not beat (so-and-so). There was an argument but then they walked out of the bar and continued into the street, they did not persue (so-and-so) in a violent act."

OF COURSE the attorney said that; he's paid to DEFEND the two. Yes, there are always 2 sides to a story, but there were witnesses!

A few said they saw and heard the quarrel, and even observed the 2 men walk out after the Red Sox fans left the bar.

In a country of justice, liberty, and a wide number of laws, when criminals can be guilty but set free and innocent individuals are convicted and sentenced to prison, what is justice, really? When politicians smile and wave but have deep, dark secrets that later come to light or when elected, turn around and run the office with different intentions... when an illegal immigrant rapes and murders a young girl and even with complete evidence (skin under the girl's fingernails, scratch marks on the immigrant), the illegal is set free just because he doesn't speak/know english and apparently doesn't know/speak spanish either, therefore he does not know the laws in this country so he is a fuckin' free man!!! I shit you not, twas in the damn news... When wealthy people can buy their way out of jail or pay a judge off to reduce their sentence...

There is no justice.

On the issue of illegal immigration, if you are an immigrant coming to America to become a U.S. citizen through documentation, and to better yourself or your life and the lives of your family and are NOT trying to hinder ▬ or ruin the lives of Americans or the state of the country itself, then I have no ▬▬▬ problem with that! check out this webpage:

Whengoodmendonothing.com/minoritystatus.
htm

Educate yourself in the abundant
crimes of illegal immigrants.

I understand if you are illegal and
are just trying to live your life. I
applaud you, just get the necessary
documents to be put on record!

And don't think I'm racist,
because I'm not.

Let's ▪ talk about sex. Let's not,
I was kidding. I am not the
typical guy who thinks about sex
every 6 seconds, or however often
it is. Sex doesn't control me
or my life, I don't crave it

How to get over the Fear of Speaking:

- Know Yourself
- Know Topic
- Know Audience
- Know Channel (energy, atmosphere)

In modeling and moreso with acting, just before a big shoot or appointment it's good to take a few minutes and use exercises to loosen up; breathe deeply, shake yourself about (no, not the hokey-pokey), stretches, screaming (if you wouldn't be booted from the place you are in), even speaking in jarble just to get the nervousness out. Laughing is another good technique.

Another sure-fire way of overcoming

fear – in any situation– is through repetition; the act of repeating an action, performance, production, or presentation. The more you do it or make yourself surrounded by your fear, the more comfortable you will be.

To the Ninja fear was just a word to describe the feeling that rises when confronted by a threat or obstacle. Someone, or many someones, may disagree to that statement. That is because we as human beings are taught since birth that fear is bad, fear is a negative emotion we feel when faced with uncertainty. It's programmed into our brains. The truth is, "Fear" is just a label, a name for a feeling, an external term for something internal. Look at all the labels we have in life, all the terms created to make life easier: Red, blue, left, right, back, front, table, rail, pen, pencil, book, top, strap, oak, mahogany, leaf, burn, tear, number, letter, cloth, thug, punk, goth, preppy, jock, nerd, geek(~~~~ ~~~~), psycho, gay, student, teacher, quiz, test, <u>body</u> language, <u>sign</u> language, ketchup, mustard, happiness, anger, tuxedo, suit. All of these are simple words that can be categorized into 2 groups:

<u>Term</u>: A word or group of words designating something, like a particular field.

<u>Label</u>: A short word or phrase descriptive of a person, group, etc.

Now, I listed more labels than terms but you get the idea. Everything in life has a name, a word that tells us what that person, place or thing is - and that is a <u>noun</u>: person, place, or thing. A label on top of a label. They make life easier. But new and bigger words are being created every year, so instead of helping us form a better understanding and ability to write and speak the language, these new words are confusing us. Have you ever read a [1]doctor's [A]<u>manual</u> or [B]<u>glossary of terms</u>? How about a guidebook to physics? I kinda understand the point, the destination, the result.... but the work in between is complex. Well, not just anybody can become a doctor or physicist. Those subjects separate the stupids from the highbrowed.

"Fear" is just a label, a name for a feeling that can be overcome given time and the right (and positive) mindset.

For example, I no longer fear walking through a dangerous neighborhood; I'm comfortable but alert, aware of my surroundings. I'm comfortable until someone or a group of people tries to hurt me or whoever I'm with.

Here's another example: I used to have slight acrophobia (fear of heights - see that word again? Fear) until I repeatedly stood atop high places and rooftops and peered out over the edge. Now I ~~am~~ no longer "fear" heights.

We, as human beings, have a right
to be happy, to live happily.

Throughout this book you may
see that I want to be happy and
I want others to be happy. So
you may think that I don't like
facing discomfort, that I dislike
unfamiliarity and I'm too sensitive
because I can't take being sad
or I throw tantrums because I'm
not happy. That is stupid and you
are naive to who you are so you are
in no position to judge me.
    Do not judge, do not assume.

I'm not judgmental, I'm analytical!
    Heh heh...

If you perceive me as weak you are deceived.

"Show weakness when you are strong and show strength when you are weak. Do this, and your opponent will underestimate you."

I'm not a bodybuilder. I don't go to a gym and religiously lift weights. I stretch before and after practicing various katas and executing my training. There are three practical exercises I perform: push-ups, sit-ups, and pull-ups. The sit-ups are of course for the toning of my abs, and the push-ups and pull-ups can be implemented into life-saving situations; possibly one day I'll have to pull myself over the edge of a roof or a cliff and back to safety. Or perhaps I'll have to push a bigger person off of me, or heavy objects? Maybe I'll go through life not needing to do any of the above.... but it does not hurt to be prepared.

Here's a little computer lingo

DSL – Digital Subscriber Lines

ISDN – Integrated Services Digital Network

ISP – Internet Service Provider

OSP – Online Service Provider

WSP – Wireless Service Provider

IP address – Internet Protocol address

Connections –

Baseband transmits one signal at a time over a phone line.
Baseband modems: 28k to 56k

Broadband transmits a vast quantity of data simultaneously.

Broadband modems: T1 ("Transmission Level 1"), DSL, cable modem, ISDN.

HTTP - Hypertext Transfer Protocol

"Far better is it to dare mighty things,
To win glorious triumphs,
Even though checkered by failure,
Than to rank with those poor
Spirits who neither
Enjoy much — Nor suffer much,
Because they live in the gray twilight
That knows either—

     Victory nor Defeat!"

         —Theodore
            Roosevelt

I'm taking Oral Communication (Speech 101) in college, along with English Composition. I don't necessarily need either class but I don't have the credits on my record, so I'll just pass with flying colors.

In Speech, I'm listening to students speak about influences in their lives and I'm not sure if anyone else noticed this, but a few students repeated an adverb twice in the same sentence. For example, "I really find what he did interesting, really," or "I actually have a band myself, actually." Watching them stand in front of the class, either they're nervous or they had no written speech to refer to — that was the case with a handful of students.

I guess that is why they're taking this class; to overcome the fear of speaking in front of an audience. A few students are improving their english as well.

Not that they *want* to take the class...the ones that aren't speaking-dominant in speaking.

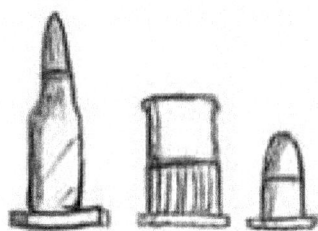

Sullivan Law— Only one son (out of two) can go into the Armed Forces; sisters and brothers can be in the same war zone, but different companies.

WWII — 450,000 soldiers died (Allied)

I see society and businesses today and I step back to view all the subjects we are constantly everyday renewing or becoming the next best thing:

- Writers = books/history
- Artists = comics/history
- Athletes = sports/history/money
- Musicians = bands/albums/money
- Singers = history/albums
- Politicians = history/new laws/rules/$$
- Actors = movies/history/$
- Inventors = the next big buck ($)/history
- Directors = blockbuster films/history
- Entrepreneurs = the next big/freedom/company/business

Everyday, all around the world, I see new faces popping up in sports, in town or city legislatures, and of course music. I see new names as the authors of books and fresh names of companies on the internet or on a billboard. In the list I created, the majority of up-and-coming stars get to where they want to make history. Others do it for the joy, the love of doing it, for the fans, for the economy, for their friends or family, or for the ones before them that inspired them to get where they want and do what they do..... but they also do it for the MONEY. The people/companies that invent a new, annoying item every year either create them to have consumers enjoy them or to make easy money off them and make people lazy. I have to agree with the latter. People are getting lazier and more impatient!

These nifty-but-naive little inventions are what they are— A WASTE OF MONEY!

A few gadgets of laziness

- Remote control
- Valet parking
- Car

Now, vehicles contradict themselves on this topic because people that have cars will drive them EVERYWHERE, thus making them out-of-shape. Then again, automobiles make traveling a HELLUVA lot easier!!!

- Remotes and valets are more of a luxury, valet parking being more of a service.

With all the paparazzis, projects, + appointments, I can understand why celebrities want houses remotely located from everyone else. They want to relax. Another reason is because with all the space, they can build their dream home the way they want.

With all my friends(family) I have now. but no crowds of fans or crazed cameramen and columnists, but still with a busy schedule, I already want to be/live alone... I'd kinda dislike to see what my life's going to be like when I'm a celebrity.....

Being famous would be a plus; I'd do movies and modeling for the connections and the money — and the fun of it.

✹ <u>Did You Know?</u>

Your stomach has to produce
a new layer of mucus every two
weeks, otherwise it will digest
itself. That's how gastric ulcers are
formed.

I will again express my personality,
hopefully to open your mind...or at
least give you insight into my deeper
self.

To put it bluntly: I am not a typical
guy. Typical as in loving to ~~go~~ go
out and drink with "the guys", watching
sports on sunday or monday nights,
or trying to "hook up" with girls at
a club, bar, or party. (If I didn't
explain the meaning of 'typical', you
probably would have thought 'typical'
is a very general statement. I

am not part of a societal mold that you can easily categorize. Do not try and say I'm like this and this unless you ~~bec~~ talk to me and dislike me for the words that come out of my mouth, dislike me upon discovering my character, my personality, because I am not an ordinary guy. To put it simply, I'm different. I'm silly, I'm serious, I'm random, I'm practical, a preacher, an artist, a teacher. A vampire, a soldier, a poet. I've had a screwed-up childhood like a bunch of people but based on my experiences in life I've changed as an individual, unlike some people who decide to stay on their path of negativity and depression. As quoted in Batman Begins: "Why do we fall? So we can learn to pick ourselves up." That's exactly what I've done in my life, continually moving toward my goals and staying loyal to my friends and family. I've tasted desperation; being homeless, asking people for money, stealing food to live, sleeping on park and cemetery benches in the cold... and I've also been through high times in my life. I've created an underground (literally) fight club with some friends, met a few kindred spirits, had poems published, and I'm friends with a number of well-known artists and a handful of celebrities. Every time my peeps and I hang out, I offer to buy them food or material possessions on behalf of them being loyal to me but also because I don't want them experiencing what I've been through, being desperate. (There are a few people I know that need to accept more responsibilities though...)

Anything else in my life is manipulated reality.... Meep!

If you don't have an open mind in this world, you might as well live in a box and be your own best friend. There are interesting people out there with ingenius ideas and intellectual views and opinions.

If you like a certain genre of music, that's fine with me as long as you don't bother me with why I like or dislike a band or singer. It's MY Life, MY Music. There is so much good music in this world. But also much CRAP.

Music $=$ Life

Music is a great therapy!

Let's not forget Love... or Art! I **love** to **draw**.

When I draw, I dive into another world and I embrace it.

I ~~love~~ enjoy creating new worlds,
new characters... I can input my
personality or the personalities of
others into my characters, I can
dream up new and exciting places, planets,
weapons, gadgets, clothing, animals,
words, vehicles, aliens... then put them
on paper and make them come alive.
When I draw, I can get lost in
my own little world. Tis amazing how
enormous my world can be within just
a handful of pages, and how the
characters or events can be
believable.

Just like when one opens a book
(preferably one that is of interest)
and becomes immersed in the story,
the protagonist, the antagonist,
EVERYTHING in the book. Everything,
everyone in the book we hold an
affinity toward, we become connected

through reading.

Same can be said with films; we start watching and eventually we build up emotions based on a situation a certain character is in or the atmosphere of the film.

Take horror films for example; with the music and impending (and sometimes inevitable) doom of the people we are watching, we as an audience know a murder is about to happen and if the tension is high and we create favorites, we hope for the best! We kinda hope a favored character lives, and many people get upset or bothered when that favorite dies. I try to be indifferent but if the movie is great and I grow to connect with someone, I am one of those people.

How I View:

My dad's lifestyle	My lifestyle
cluttered, somewhat disorganized, no discipline, arrogant	organized, disciplined, open-minded, reserved

A q 1 2   A   q 1   2

- Description of lines on next page -

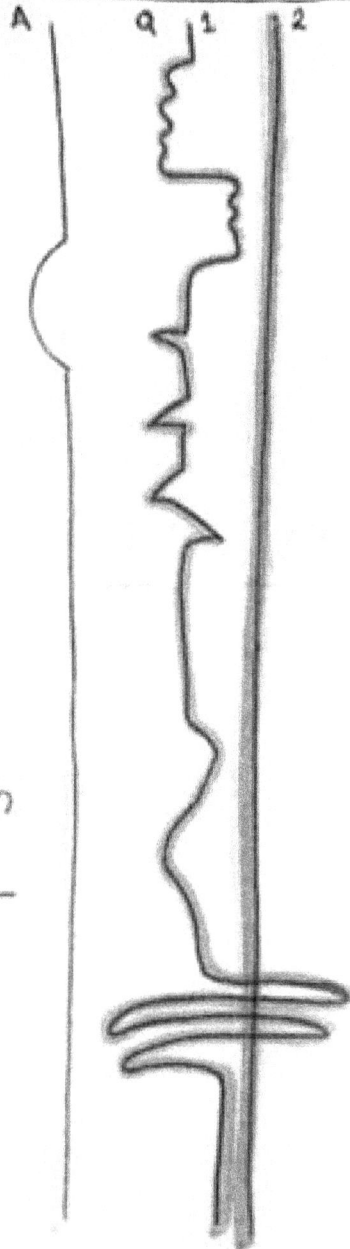

LINE A: Way of living physically, standard of living. How one performs tasks and how they are accomplished — fast, messy as opposed to controlled, patient.

LINE Q1: Way of thinking, either receptive or nonreceptive to new ideas and information. Open-minded as opposed to narrow-minded.

LINE Q2: Mindset; one's views so decided upon, so powerfully established. A certain behavior(s) and choice(s) that one lives by. "Cognitive bias", also described as 'mental inertia.'

The poet John Keats created a theory called "negative capability". It is expressed as such:

"Keats believed that great people (especially poets) have the ability to accept that not everything can be resolved. Keats was a Romantic and believed that the truths found in the imagination access holy authority. Such authority cannot be 'understood', and thus he writes of 'uncertainties.' This 'being in uncertainty' is a place between the mundane, ready reality and the multiple potentials of a more fully understood existence."

Work cited:

"Negative-capability." Wikipedia, the free encyclopedia. 21 Nov. 2007. Reference.com http://www.reference.com/browse/wiki/Negative_capability>.

Is it worse to live without a purpose,
or to die without a cause?

What is the deal with shoppers taking their groceries out to their cars, then leaving the shopping carts to roll into another car or sticking them right behind (or in front, depending on the direction the vehicle is facing) another person's vehicle? Either people are=

* Lazy, and don't feel like walking the cart all the way to its holding cell

* Don't want to leave their kids unattended in their vehicle, especially if the keys are in the ignition

* Feel it is not their job, and the employees can do it

or

* Have some place to go, someone to

There have been a number of times I have seen an individual leave their cart in an empty parking spot next to their car, just to have the cart roll into the vehicle in the next spot over. Some people walk over, check the side of the vehicle, and upon noticing there is only a scratch or no damage at all, will prop the cart onto the curb (which should have been done in the first place!) then get into their car, truck, SUV, whatever and drive off.....
Others will just look around and continue on their way.......

pricks.

More people need
patience. The ones
that don't have it or
have little of it feel,
"If others don't have
it, why should I?"
That's the ignorance
and impatience to learn
that _more_ people _need_
less of.
It is said, "If you
can't beat 'em, join 'em."
Right? WRONG! I feel
you should change yourself,
be different from the
indifferent ones!

I would rather face a
whole army of people and
die on my own two feet.

It would not matter if
you read this from front
to back, back to front,
or random sections at a
time; this book is random
and there are no chapters.
This book is my streaming flow
of consciousness.
It is existence through my
EYES.
Life how I'm living it.
The universe how I see it,
how I feel it.

Just by picking up this
book and reading something
out of it, you have thrown
away your understanding of
this so-called reality, at
least temporarily (unless you
learn something and apply it to

your life).

I don't like shaving but I strongly dislike facial hair... so I have to choose the better of two evils.

When you live a certain way, or exercise/work out a certain way, for a long while, enough to make it become a habit, your body becomes attuned to the routine. When you change that routine and immediately try to live/exercise a different way, the human body is not used to the sudden change, it needs to adapt to the habit. Your body remembers just as much as your brain, but while you think of the memory with your brain, of course your body REMEMBERS by feeling. Not many people know that our bodies remember. We feel a certain texture with our fingers or we wear a nice, comfy jacket or hoodie, and we _think_ our minds remember that feeling, and they do. But our bodies also remember that feeling, that touch.

I was taught in middle school (Grades 6-8) to never say "a lot" or "lots of" in a sentence, whether on paper or in speech. Of course we don't truly heed that "never," but it is good to train yourself to use "a bunch" or "bunches of," or "large numbers of," "a number of," "large amount," even terms like "numerous" or "abundance." Doing so will increase your proficiency in speaking and communication overall.

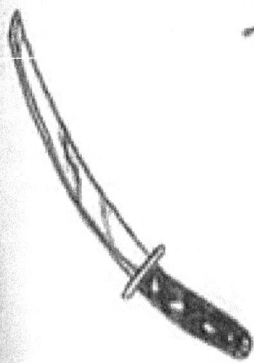

The term 'Bushido', which is the Samurai code of honor they lived by (and the code that I live by, with a modern touch), can be split into two characters as well as three.

武 士 道

BU　　　SHI　　　DO

'Bu' translates as <u>War</u> or <u>martial</u>
'Shi = <u>Warrior</u>
'Do' = <u>Way</u>
    Bu · shi · do
It can also be split into 2 parts:
    Bushi · do
Bushi = <u>samurai</u>, <u>warrior</u>　Do = <u>Way</u>

Have you heard it's physically impossible to lick your elbow? Well how about these facts:

A snail can sleep for three years.

"Go," is the shortest complete sentence in the English language.

A duck's quack doesn't echo.

The duck's quack is a strange one, and I bet you looked at your elbows, contemplating whether or not to ~~try~~ try and lick them huh? OR maybe you really did try to lick them...... unless programmed (taught) otherwise, humans are curious creatures and if one is told NOT to look at a certain website or open a magazine to a specific page, they will be thinking of what that page or that site holds. Most of the time that person will be so curious they'll find out what is so 'gross' or 'bad'........

Curiosity killed the cat, not the dog right?

..... then they'll be grossed-out or disturbed, some people laugh about it, then they'll tell someone else not to view it, ⌐ and that's how it is spread, like a poison running through your veins!

So <u>do not</u> visit lemonparty.org or tubgirl.com! Don't log onto a site and search for the video, "2 girls, 1 cup."

Don't do it!

A fortune I received with a cookie:

Today is the tomorrow we worried about yesterday.

It is said that orange peels are great helpers in preventing various diseases including cancer and heart disease. I recently tried orange peel. While eating the orange, I bit off a piece of the peel and started to chew. It wasn't bad.... but I think it would've been better if I ate the ~~outside~~ outside with the inside.

Other than orange skin, other peels that are super-duper healthy are apple skin (who doesn't eat apple skin?) and pomegranate skin, but pomegranates are excellent for you anyway: in the form of juice, nutrition bars, or the seeds.

The next handful of pages are blank for the enjoyment/therapy of your life, your day, your week, your minute. They are blank for one to write in thoughts, pet peeves, or to vent an emotion. The pages can contain words, pictures, or colors — ANYTHING! You can write how much you hate this book if it makes you feel better. ☺

Vent, poeticize, randomize...

America

Is run on debt (period)

Consumerism helps make money to run things and that's part of what keeps the cash flowing, thus persuading consumers to buy more, spend more and have little to take care of oneself to buy food or pay necessary bills. Unless one is smart with their money.

- Make a budget.
- Save money.
- Be punctual with paying bills.
- Pay more than the interest/minimum on a credit card
- Be careful with credit cards
- Consolidate loans
- Spend on what is important first, <u>then</u> splurge

← Follow these guidelines and it will help you stay out of debt!

"Less than all things, men must grudge money: it is by riches that wisdom is hindered."

←

←

Last night I was waiting for Mike to pick me up at the UA where I used to work, so we could see a movie at IMAX. I drew a face tattoo on myself earlier, before I went to the theater... and as I was waiting for Mike, this one kid hanging out with a few of his friends in the lobby told me, "Hey, your tattoo is cracked."

I kind of thought he said "crap" so I didn't reply, so he said it again. I asked him, "Did you say it was "crap" or "cracked?"

He replied, "Cracked."

I guessed that meant 'cool' or 'wicked,' but I just said, "Oh."

Then he turned to his friends and I heard him ask them rhetorically, "What, he doesn't know what 'cracked' means?"

HOLD THE PHONE! STOP

THE PRESSES! Sorry, I do not know what 'cracked' means in their sense of the word, nor have I even _heard_ it in that sense.... if words liked "cracked" are in the vocab. of youth today, boy do they have it different (in a bad way). When I was growing up, "cool" or "nice" or "awesome" were words of complimentary expression. Heck no, I don't know what "cracked" means in your terms, let alone do I even care!

Anything similar I have been trying to start for a future generation is the word "shway" for "cool." I'd rather hear shway! than cracked!!!

What if, instead of saying, "I hate" or "We hate", we said "I hurt" or "We hurt?" Hate is a strong word. For example, "I hurt to see you go!" Of course, it won't sound right if we say, "I hurt you," or "I hurt "that movie," but the use of the word is understood.

"I hurt to have that happen."

———

You don't have to be religious to be spiritual.

You don't have to be wealthy to be happy.

You don't have to see to believe.

enin learned to read when he was 5 years old. He entered school at the age of 9 in 1879, and became a brilliant student.

Lenin was a brilliant man. So was Hitler, minus his military strategies. He was big into art and architecture, but his goal was so negative. Starting a genocide of a race because they're not blonde with blue eyes is definitely immoral.

Same with the swaztika; it is very profound, a simple and appealing symbol, but it was/is used for an extremely dastard cause.
The reverse of the swaztika stands for "Peace" in Chinese. 卐 = "SS"
卍 = "Peace"

"Whatever you can do or dream you can do, begin it. Boldness has genius and power and magic in it."

Yang

Yin

Everything has a balance, Everything needs a balance. The "yin" to a "yang". If something is too hot, it burns. If something is too cold, it freezes. The same goes for driving on a highway; too fast, one can cause an accident. Drive too slow, it can also cause an accident. If you receive, also should you give. It is better to give than to receive, and I agree. I enjoy seeing the expressions on the faces I give to. Be grateful for what you receive. Be grateful for who and what you have in life.

Can you still breath?
Can you still walk?
Can you still see?
hear?
taste?
smell?

I want you to stop for a moment, and think of the people you have in your life, think of the privileges given to you. Do you ~~have~~ have clothing on you? Do you have a roof over your head when you sleep? Do you have food in your stomach? Not everyone is as fortunate as you.

I know very well a number of people that have gone or are going through a really tough time in their lives.

Take my friend Steve: He's an accident like I am, his birth wasn't planned. He doesn't have a father and he moved out of his mom's house because he was _sick_ and _tired_ of her ranting, ridicule, and sick of being the one yelled at every day. I can relate with the ranting and raving, my dad is the same way.
Now Steve is homeless, living in a shelter with others. It is not a place to take lightly when you can't trust the person next to you, while you're sleeping or awake.

Here's another person: she's more of an acquaintance now than a friend but she's been raped, her parents are getting divorced, she's been on the street (homeless, _not_ prostitute), and there have been former jobs she's left because of sexual harassment. One job, her manager told her he'd fire her if she didn't have sex with him! The only friends she knows are either homeless (after being kicked out of their houses at 18) or have homes but no jobs. One may look at her situation and think, "she's a druggie," and I will say that she has done drugs before and she used to drink, but she's desperately trying to change her life. The problems are, she's trying too hard... and she makes friends/knows the wrong people. One may say she can live with one of her parents but how can she if her parents don't want her? I tell her she needs to move out of her environment, move to a new, better town but it's difficult when she has no money.

This girl used to cut herself to deal

with her problems, but now she's smarter than that and actually DEALS with her obstacles. They say, if you can make it in New York, you can make it anywhere. Tis true; New York is competitive in terms of modeling, acting, careers, and corporations (although corporations go unsaid, they're self-explanatory). The state of New York is also challenging. When I say challenging, isn't it obvious what I is talking about?! Life. No, not the board game, not the cereal. Life. The existence of a human being. Life in New York is great because it has everything here - movie stars, film industry, fashion industry, and a large number of a wide variety of people (mostly in the city). On the contrary, life in New York is not that great. Especially on Long Island. Homeless kids, drug dealers, young teens killing another over something so small and stupid, a large abundance of illegal immigrants, immature (utterly stupid and pointless) gang initiations, the high cost of living due to high taxes and expensive houses and apartments, arrogant, ignorant, and uneducated, close-minded people—both young, old, and inbetween— and let me conclude with the disgustingly hot and humid summers! I may be speaking my opinion of the weather, but there are plenty of people I know who can agree.

As much as that acquaintance of mine asks for my help, I've helped her enough years ago and she was okay... but it seems, as much as I try and as much advice as I give her, she does not heed what I suggest. Then what else is there to do? I suggested she read life-changing books. I'm not sure she'll do it. She is too focused on the negative that she sees and experiences, she won't believe anything that's not physical, like religious or spiritual faith. The thing is, the life-changing book doesn't have to be either/or. It can be just that — life-changing! I wish her the best, along with anybody else going through hard times. Just know that you are not alone.

If a kind lady didn't invite Steve over to have a nice, warm and fulfilling dinner on a certain holiday, I would have. There are many more to come.

P.S. - In Long Island, New York, if you don't have an adequate support system or you're not wealthy enough to live comfortably, it is difficult to live. Is that everywhere though? I don't know, it's just depressing here.

"Have compassion for all beings, rich and poor alike; each has their suffering. Some suffer too much, others too little."

If I don't put quotes around a proverb that means I wrote it... same w/ a poem.

(throughout this whole book)

"Life isn't about finding yourself. Life is about <u>creating</u> yourself."
—unknown

I have to half agree with this quote; many people do not have a sense of identity and therefore look for one on the journey of creating themselves.

✳ Don't be a collector, be a renter. Do not collect debt, rent it. Do not collect unnecessary, unwanted objects and papers... rent. If the paper holds useful information and the time comes to need it, search for it on the internet. If the world wide web is not available at the time, that is why we have a brain, to remember things. If you get cenile or contract alzheimer's, find the information then write it, print it, record it any way. I know this wouldn't be fair to the ones that are computer illiterate.

Don't convert people, invert them. Help them find themselves and find within them completion and enlightenment.

Courtesy · Kindness · Clarity
Compassion · Mediation · Meditation · Completion
Right decision · Realisation

"There is importance in every breath."

Divinity
Unity
Trinity
Infinity

I don't hate people, I just look down upon the characteristics of the ones that feel they have to prove to everyone else that they're better or they can do something better. Although a few factors can be they grew up with an inferiority complex because of their parents, teachers or bullies, or bosses... you should not need to prove anything to ANYONE, but yourself. Don't care what others think of you.

If you are negatively influenced by others and change everything you are, just to please those who influenced you, are you happy 'cause you fit in? What if they change and they don't like you anymore? Are you going to change yourself yet again or art thou going to kill yourself? Don't find a clique or gang. Find yourself! Don't kill yourself, don't

give up, kill the negative influence.
Kill the need to fit in. LIVE your
life.

Make a commitment. Set
your aim. Go for it.

Start a new habit. A good
habit. A beneficial habit.

"It is easier to change the world than
to adapt to it."

(Unless you're lazy and don't mind
being part of the bland design that
doesn't change anything or make things
happen.)
My friend Kevin told me "conformity is
hard to break away from." Not if yoos a
                              misfit!

Watching Juno, a Fox Searchlight picture,
and seeing/hearing aboot similar
situations in life having to do with the
break-up of the foster parents, I
have come to realize the generic
being of men over the past years and
of today:

A man and woman get married. They
are happy for a time. When the woman
decides to have a child, the man decides
he is not ready to be a father and
wants to part from the relationship
and either find someone else or
continue persuing a childhood dream (if
that dream was never reached.) The
woman has the baby and raises her
child with a new spouse or on her own.
The split can also happen after having
the kid, or multiple kids. Neither
parent is happy because of the other,
or one isn't happy because of the
work load of the kids and/or their job.

That is the cause of many problems:
NOT BEING HAPPY
or
NOT BEING CONTENT WITH ONE'S LIFE
and
NOT BEING FULFILLED

Whether it is because of having an unexpected child or the standard of living in a certain environment, or the lack of will and resources. If by choice that it's a lack of will, that is your fault and if you don't change, you are your own downfall.

I know it is difficult but you have to blame yourself. Go on, take the blame. Not many people do.

I don't see the point of arguing about what's the better sex, both genders are paramount and required for the survival of the species. When it comes to what gender is more attractive that's a matter of opinion; in my eyes girls are more attractive, more physically appealing... but I say that 'cause I is a guy. When the decision is about which can take more pain— it is said guys can. That is half true. Of course it depends on the person, how skinny or big they are ...and it depends on their pain threshold (if any). Guys can take more punches and scrapes and cuts, but girls can withstand more pain when it comes to childbirth.... and I'm not too sure males can give birth! If anyone tells me girls are more sensitive emotionally, that too is half right. Guys are sensitive as well, it depends on the person. There are some girls that aren't sensitive at all. Yes, guys cheat on their spouses (a bunch), but so do a bunch of girls. Girls gossip but so do a handful of guys. There are smart girls and there are smart boys. IT DOESN'T MATTER WHAT GENDER; so don't be sexist!

I like to explore. I'm curious. I like to have my eyes open to many things. That's one reason how I have acquired a sense of identity and accumulated a wealth of understanding— I have an open mind.

That may well be in part due to my Scorpio nature but it is also a result of having much freedom. :)

Random — Farting means you're healthy

The "rule" of drinking 8 glasses of water to keep yourself hydrated is definitely not true! It depends on the person (age, activity level, physical condition) and the climate.
About coffee drying out your skin, that's not true as well.

I feel a spike in my [joy] emotion every time a *girl I find attractive calls me "hun" or "sweetie" ~~and~~ and actually means it. My [happiness] rises quickly every time that happens, if I am happy to begin with. If I'm not, hearin it shoots my mood up, even if a little. What I enjoy more is hearing it from a significant other or a girl I'm pursuing, and it means that much more coming from that specific person.

Tis similar to a shot of adrenaline, the warm feeling rising in my body.

* That girl is either a friend or celebrity I've had a crush on.

† It seems a large number of men don't grow up as quickly as a large number of women. But that can be applied to women as well, just refer to Stephanie Condron's article later in this book.

Don't be biased/sexist

I just completed an online test to discover which side of my brain is dominant. Of course the Test is not fully accurate but it comes damn close! The Test gave highly accurate-but-somewhat-wrong psychological traits of myself (A handful of interpretations were right-on while a select few were almost true).

Although my brain is almost evened out, I am:

52% Left Brained
48% Right Brained

My Left Brain	My Right Brain
53% Sequential	44% Fantasy-oriented
47% Reality based	29% Intuitive
25% Logical	28% Concrete
20% Verbal	24% Holistic
17% Symbolic	19% Nonverbal
11% Linear	17% Random

Left Brain, Right Brain processing percentages.

"You create your own universe as you go along."

— Marlon Brando

PVC – polyvinyl chloride

I don't understand the English language at times; "often" is spelled with a "t" but it's pronounced "offen"... so many people say it that way and I just find it annoying. Letters shouldn't be silent unless it's a name! Offen sounds like a fish...

Either way, I'm with you all the way.

↑ I told this to Leon when he was contemplating the start of our day.

Money itself isn't bad, it's the <u>love</u> of money that produces Greed. Money is important in the world today, it's a tool/commodity, but let money consume you and you'll transform into a self-important, cocky bastard. I pity the individuals that have sugar daddies and sugar mommies, they have to be missing something in their lives... unless they were <u>born</u> with money in their ▬▬▬ hands.

Don't wait meditate. 🧘 Or... get in a session of accupuncture and accupressure every month or so... providing you have the finances for that! Meditation's free.

"Tomorrow is the most important thing in life. It's perfect when it arrives and it puts itself in our hands. It hopes we've learned something from yesterday."

                          - John Wayne

When reading aboot video games in magazines and the internet, it's so great to ~~know~~ read/hear the new features in a sequel to a certain blockbuster game ... but when the game is released, you discover the rumors were so much better than the actual finished product.

Check this out: for breakfast I ate Waffles, orange slices, and a plum, but after I had a bunch of green grapes and drank orange juice, I had an aftertaste of raisins in my mouth... pretty cool.

"Whoah. No wealth. I'd just want your time and company lol."

Thanks Amber...

© For years, this is what we've all seen or experienced in and out of high school:

A guy wants to be with a certain girl, the girl doesn't want that guy because he's younger or around the same age as she is. The girl wants an older guy.

Here's another situation, in or out of school:

Someone (guy or girl) wants Friend 1. Friend 1 doesn't want that Someone, they want Friend 2, but Friend 2 wants Potential 1. Hardly anybody gets who they want sometimes.

Just take a moment to think of the enormous abundance of bands in <u>every</u> state, every country, all the on-going websites from around the world, think of all the books getting published yearly from this country to the next.

Now isn't THAT a
number?

FACT: The largest mall in the world is the West Edmonton Mall in Alberta, Canada, which has 828 stores. The parking lot holds 20,000 cars.

— IMPORTANT —

Stephanie Condron writes in the Daily Mail on August 2, 2004, "Turning eighteen is the milestone birthday that traditionally marks the passage from adolescence to adulthood. But it seems many of us are taking much longer to really grow up." Stephanie has cited research from the UK and the United States referring to tests of adulthood, ranging from leaving home to becoming financially independent. She reports that, "the teenage years seem to be stretching well into the 30s" and "fewer 30-year-olds can really be considered adults."

The research shows that in 1960, 65 percent of males and 70 percent of females over 18 could be regarded as having passed the tests for adulthood.

Today, the figures are 46% for males, and 25% for females.

+ The average lead pencil will draw a line 35 miles long or write approximately 50,000 English words. +

My friend Ian came to a bright conclusion: if he is in debt, why not be in debt taking part in something he enjoys doing/<u>wants</u> to do. This is in reference to continuing education in his ideal field of study.

Whose idea was it to put an 's' in the word "lisp?"

"It is in changing that we find purpose."

Get this: In cats, an organ on the roof of their mouth (called the vomeronasal organ) connects to the nasal cavity and allows cats to essentially taste what they smell. That is how cats distinguish if food is fresh enough for their liking.

Countries, like America, are failing economically. America is failing economically, politically, and given the events of hypocritical priests who fondle young boys and the news stories of 9 year-old boys raping a 12 year-old girl, and a mother burning the skin off her child in a boiling-hot bath tub, America is failing ethically (on top of plenty of other dastardly-defective deeds around the nation).

America is failing ethically?! What am I saying?.... There are tons of other countries that are the same way, if not worse.

On the President Day weekend of February 16-18, I felt like being spontaneous. Without planning it, I took half my paycheck and went up to Buffalo, New York.

Upon returning to Manhattan, on the ride down I met a cool girl that is going to FIT and someday planning to start her own fashion clothing line.

I'm here in Penn station waiting for the 3:16 AM train back, and since my butt has been sitting in a cramped seat for 7 hours, I was walking around and bought a sandwich and a drink. Since I had no cash and only the money in my debit account, I asked if there was a minimum for a debit transaction. Since I already had a drink and I wasn't about to eat another sandwich, I asked a guy standing outside the store if he was hungry. After he replied with an appreciative no, I still didn't feel like buying more than I wanted for myself. I asked if he was thirsty, and if he wanted to have something for later. He picked out a drink and I bought the drink and my samich. The guy was really happy, very appreciative, and thanked me. He had a geniune spark of gratitude in his face, and that made me happy. I didn't know if he was homeless but I didn't care much; from the Port Authority to Penn, I was asked if I could spare some money and feeling bad for not having the charitable funds, I was glad to still do a good deed, whether or not that guy really wanted anything.

Seeing how happy he was made my night. So did the fact I was finally off that bus!

Did you know? The Boy Scouts were founded February 8, 1910.

CARBON

- Carbon is used for strong and light-weight products

- Time and special machinery form carbon into specific shapes

- Strength-to-weight ratio in sports cars is second-to-none.

- Rare + Expensive

It's difficult and challenging living in the world today. I guess it's always been though, hasn't it?!

Futuristic concept cars to keep an eye out for (or to add to interesting stories): Mazda Taiki, Suzuki Pixy, Toyota Rin, Honda Puyo, Toyota FT-HS, Toyota CS&S, Toyota Volta, Toyota 1/X, Acura Advanced Sports Car, Aston Martin Rapide, Audi RSQ (used in the film 'I, Robot' from 20th Century Fox), Audi Nero, AV Design Forte, Cadillac Sien (Spanish for 100), Chrysler ecoVoyager, Chrysler ME412, Citroen C-Metisse (Mongrel in French), Citroen C-Airlounge, EDAG No. 8 (I'm not into convertibles but I LOVE the color!), Ferrari F250, Ferrari F460 Tifosi, Ford SYNus — so much WOW! factor, HBK Saar 276 Concept, Honda REMIX, Hyundai HCD10 Hellion, IED beON, Infiniti Coupe Concept, Lamborghini Ferrucchio, Maserati Birdcage 75th, Maybach Exelero, Mazda Sassou (in Japanese, "Sassou" means optimism for the future, having a positive state of mind), Mazda Nagare (Japanese for "Flow"), Mazda Ryuga (Japanese for "gracious flow"), Mini BioMoke, Mitsubishi EZ MIEV, Mitsuoka

Orochi, Nike One, Nissan Terranaut, Nissan NV200, Nissan Intima, Nissan Zaroot, Opel Flextreme, Opel GTC (Gran Turismo Coupe), Peugeot Moovie, Peugeot Hoggar, Peugeot 4002, Kia Sidewinder, Renault Twingo, Renault Raccoon, Rinspeed Senso (not so much the outside, mostly the design and innovative monitoring of the interior), Suzuki Kizashi, Suzuki Mobile Terrace (which is somewhat evident in Japanese animes), Nuno Teixeira MYBUS, Volkswagen Nanospyder, Volkswagen IROC, and the Splinter - a new and unique concept for any vehicle; the Splinter is a graduate project at North Carolina State University comprising almost fully of wood. Check out how it's being done:

www.joeharmondesign.com

I have read many astounding ~~things~~ discoveries: robots evolving (learning how to lie), the study and experimentation of teleporting atoms, and how the extinction of the honeybee would put a damper on ice cream, as well as a large number of businesses and fruits.

Knowledge is power — or so they say. Knowing something is very important, but being able to apply it to a situation in life is paramount. It also depends on what kind of knowledge I is talking about; insight and understanding that's good to know, or substantial practicality. Another form of knowledge can be useless information but some of that can be good to know as well.

"At some point, the choice you will face is whether to carry out your duties or live your life."

RULE 34

—

"If it exists, there is porn of it."

RULE 36

—

"If it exists, someone has a fetish for it."

These are rules of the internet

One's mind is influenced and created by its growing environment. Get a child young enough and the possibilities are very abundant in raising him/her.

- Instead of burning or chopping up old tires, several companies can effectively break down old tires into components that can be recycled and reused. Those components are oil, carbon black, and steel.

- Tuberculosis, or TB, is contracted from eating contaminated meat, poor nutrition, or inhalation of respiratory droplets. For example, if someone infected with TB were to sneeze or cough, a person(s) can get the disease by breathing in the surrounding dust or droplets that contain the bacteria.

- The trick with a credit card wedged into a door frame to unlock the door, like in movies, really works... except it takes a considerably longer time to do the act than in the movies.

- Toyota is developing a new ethanol production capability which will enable biofuel to be obtained from wood chips, unlike today's biofuels which are made from food crops.

Once scientists state something is good for you, like eating chocolate before bed to help improve sleep, later down the road research on the same topic will state what they said was good for you, is now bad for you.

The same works in reverse; a diet in a specific food or playing too much video games can, at first, be bad until researchers come out with saying it is now good. Video games are said to increase hand-eye coordination; that's not to say it's beneficial to play 24/7, exercise is key to staying healthy.

"Common sense is not so common."
    — Voltaire

You would think when an individual gets to college, they will have the decency and maturity to clean up after themselves. Some students leave trash on tables they were sitting at, others wash their hands and upon throwing out the paper towels, they will drop one and not even bother to pick it up. I know I'm getting into etiquette here, but most people I see don't even accomplish a simple task such as pushing in their chairs. They simply can't be bothered. The problem with most people is, they don't care... unless they have a complex about people doing things for them, making them feel better than others or more "important" than the average bear.

"Responsibility for our future lies on our own shoulders."
  — the Dalai Lama

(Say this slowly) Plumbs for thumbs...
       It sounds funny.

I was overhearing two girls at school discuss pregnancies. One of them said <u>not</u> to have a summer pregnancy, because she had tons of ice cream, water bottles, and slurpees to devour. "It's not fun."

The scent of your hair,
So sweet, ████ ████ so sweet
I breathe in memories,
I look in your eyes
Don't look away just yet,
Not yet
I've found the moment
To make me content

Many times I feel I am too contemplative; I'll think of an action or deed to do and on the way to do that deed or in the middle of doing that action my mind thinks, "This needs to get done" or "Before I do, I should put this here or pick this up." In that split second that thought comes up, my body hesitates and I think to myself, "I can do that _after_ what I originally planned to do," so I just spent 2 seconds standing/sitting in place... when I do this it annoys me. My brain is thinking really fast and my body says, "Okay, let's do that." Bastard body...

I am here at the Chicago airport waiting for my connecting flight to LAX (Los Angeles) and I look around — so many people are eating McDonald's! Everyone that _is_ eating is eating McDonald's. Booo. And as

I look around, the laptop of choice is a Mac. Macs and McDonald's. I wouldn't be surprised if they paid people to market their brands. In movies there is nothing more annoying than brand marketing — other than bad acting or the total mismaking of a video game or comic book movie!

Yes, people like something to eat that is fast and cheap. And then there are ones that don't want to spend the time and effort to make something or deal with the mess.

Aaagh! People always go for the window or aisle seats! Nobody wants the bitch seat, sitting inbetween two people. They either want to have a scenic flight or have leg and arm room. At first I didn't mind being the man in the middle but seeing the middle seat open often, it itches the back of my mind.

A sonic boom produced by a bullet traveling above the speed of sound (approximately 1,087 feet per second) cannot be silenced by a firearm suppressor.

The 15th day of April 2008, today, I went to Marvel Entertainment, Inc. in the city for an interview. As a little kid I dreamed of drawing comics... and today I was standing in and taking a tour of the Marvel Comics offices! Just last week I took a tour of EALA (Electronic Arts Los Angeles) in PlayaVista, California. My game design professor told his class that comics and video games aren't dreams, they're goals. I see that that is true, as long as ~~one~~ one keeps a positive mindset, has a strong drive and enough persistence they can make that dream a reality.

WHEREVER LIFE TAKES YOU, JUST LOOK FOR THE SIGNS

Desirea Noker
Psychologist
+ (actress)

Alex Castro
race car driver

Steve Southwell
video game developer
and artist - All Aspects!

Julio Castro
alternative fuel technician

Matthew Marino
The bother, the friend,
to help them all.

IMPOSSIBLE IS NOTHING

James Tasso
Founder of AlphaOmega
Productions, Filmmaker,
editor

Patty Thielemier
musician, writer

Jeremy Marino
Storyteller,

Michelle Mosco
Photographer +
Ruler of all worlds!

Information assurance
agent
Social Engineer

Nick "DeHero"
3D Modeller

REVOLUTIONIST!

On the train to Jamaica, Queens, we passed by a store that was named "99¢ Dreams." It sounds like they sell cheap and short wet dreams, or you can aptly buy dreams or fantasies if you have no creativity or unconscious adventures of your own. Heh heh.

+ Every year traffic worsens, more and more cars appear on the road. Same with trains; this year of 2008 trains are packed with bodies at almost every hour except the wee hours of mid-AM. The MTA stated they were going to double the number of trains that arrive and leave from Jamaica. They should get on that sooner than the projected date given.

With more people traveling in and out of Penn station, there's no need to have a fare hike — there's always going to be a constant, if not steady flow of passengers. If the

trains, tracks, ▬▬ or stations need
maintenance, that is why ∧have high
                           we
taxes! ⌣ "Thank you Uncle Sam" +

Multilingualism is the ▬▬▬▬ occurrence
or ability to use or speak two or more
languages. A generic term for a multilingual
person is a polyglot.
In the comics universe, the power of
Omni-linguism is the ability to ▬▬▬ understand any form of language. That would be
cool (and useful!) to have!

Cintra, a durable plastic, can be molded when pouring hot water on it, thus making it pliable.

My horoscope for today

New methods of talking about your feelings can offer you a chance to relate to others differently, but it won't be easy. Just don't forget that there is a fine line between maintaining your position with determination and being overly rigid. But nothing will be gained by just giving up. As paradoxical as this may sound, hold on to your vision while simultaneously remaining flexible.

I'm not enormously into astrology like some peeps, but I do follow my horoscopes every now and again; ~~the~~ ~~best~~ ~~part~~ the majority of times they're right about my day or week and my mood.

WHEN you is on the phone with a customer service representative, and you are trying to pay a bill or sort out questions/solve a problem, don't you strongly dislike it when the customer service rep might be new, still in training? They either sound like they are reading off the screen or from the paper they are given to learn their answers and customer service pitches/intros. They try and sound as professional as possible but stutter, answer with an "uhh," or there's a 3-second pause after a complexing question you hope you can receive a simple answer to.

Do you wish to speak to someone in charge, a supervisor of the department or higher? Don't you always think, "Why did I have to get a new guy?" And you hope for somebody more experienced the next time you call?

Most of the time when a person calls

(flip)

customer service, they will get that rep. who is in training or who is at least less experienced than you would like. And then there are the _good_ ones who can help you through anything you need.
Is there anything █████ else you need help with?
"Nope, thank you very much."
"Okay, thank you for calling, you have a nice day!"

████ Tis really annoying talking to someone from a collections agency, their job is not only to set up a payment plan with you or collect the debt you one, their job also consists of being a d!ck to you in the nicest way.

• Indifference
• Professionally bad attitude
• Constantly repeating your amount past due

(service with a smile)

A <u>fortune</u> I have out of the <u>500</u>:
"When you gather all *your resources together, goals are accomplished."

I really don't have 500 fortunes saved

Astronomer James Lick, who died in 1876, is buried in the base of the telescope at Lick Observatory in California.

"Today is the tomorrow we worried about yesterday."

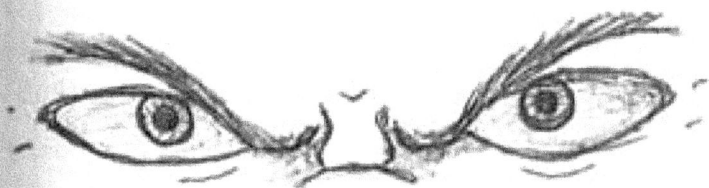

Do not falter, do not stray.
Leave my presence to find your way.

Sound Levels

Decibel level	Example
30	Quiet library, soft whispers
40	Living room, refrigerator, bedroom away from traffic
50	Light traffic, normal conversation, quiet office
60	Air conditioner at 20 feet, sewing machine
70	Vacuum cleaner, hair dryer, noisy restaurant
80	Average city traffic, garbage disposals, alarm clock at 2 feet
The	following noises can be dangerous under constant exposure
90	Subway, motorcycle, truck traffic, lawn mower.
100	Garbage truck, chainsaw, pneumatic drill
120	Rock band concert in front of speakers, thunderclap
140	Gunshot, jet plane
180	Rocket-launching pad

Don't allow others to build a
certain comfort level in conversation
with you; you don't know if they'll
talk to others about you behind your
back despite you or just because
they like to talk. (And people like to talk)

"Live in New York, but move before
you get too hard. Live in Northern
California, but move before you get
too soft."

My friends are family, and so are
my pets! Eri's take on having kids
was simply put: "I don't want kids,
I want pets." Of course that doesn't
mean subjecting children to the same
conditions as a cat, dog, or some
other domesticated animal.

Doug Liman's 'Jumper' flick is not quite realistic as stated by physicists, but wouldn't it be nice if we could tear a hole in time and space, and travel to any place on this earth? For Jumper's physics, Liman said it's like opening a door from one room to another.

Edward Farhi, the director of the Center for Theoretical Physics at MIT stated breakthroughs in physics have allowed a particle to be teleported up to 2 miles. To move a human is a different matter; "We would have to destroy the actor," Farhi said in a panel at MIT as they dissected the film's take on science. On referring to Farhi's "destroying the actor" bit, "quantum teleportation" is said to be the most realistic and possible means of teleportation. The theory is not as simple as "classical teleportation" as seen in Star Trek, but has more to do with transporting the particles of a person rather than the person's body.

Let me break the process down into easy-to-understand terms:

Teleporting a person through quantum

means is like faxing a document or image from one location to another, except with different ink and paper at the other end. From Point A the information of the atoms, the molecular "property," is copied and recreated at Point B — in other words, the person being teleported would die at Point A and be reincarnated at Point B.

There is a complication though; this process would destroy the original body, consequently subtracting the person's soul. A doppelganger would be created and both bodies would be lifeless.

Charles Bennett of IBM Research, part of the team that first discovered "quantum teleportation," believes it is feasible to teleport humans without resorting to the complexities of quantum entanglement, at least in principle. Bennett ~~explains~~ explains, "Quantum entanglement is valuable in transmitting particles such as atoms and photons where the most delicate properties are significant and where simple approximation is not enough."

He goes on to observe, "Everything we know about biology and how molecules fit together to produce a living being, including the brain, indicates that creating some level of approximation would give you a real person who was a serviceable replica of the original, in terms of looking the same and thinking the same thoughts, without necessarily being a perfect quantum replica.

"The teleported person would end up slightly different, but not in a biologically important way."

"It's the same but not the same."

"What might be possible in theory is, from a technological point of view, blatantly impossible," he says. "If you consider all the atoms in a person, and the fact that in the scan you would have to locate all those atoms to within a nanometer of each other, and then have some machine capable of translating that information into DNA, water, fat, protein, etc. — it's just silly to think about."

Ray Bradbury, a popular and very prolific writer of science fiction, always wanted to be a playwright. He would spend his days in the library instead of going to school. One of the best lines he has ever said, and one everyone should remember, is "Be your own person. Don't listen to anyone else. You must love what you do and do what you love."

"Be careful to whom you listen."

"Once you know how to read and write, you know how to think."

Again:

"Be your own person. Don't listen to anyone else. You must love what you do and do what you love."

Some of the best advice for one to remember!

RANDOM FACT

The human heart creates enough pressure when it pumps out to the body to squirt blood 30 feet.

<u>xenophobia</u> - The fear or hatred of strangers or foreigners

<u>sinophobe</u> - person with a fear of anything associated with China (This is sort of a funny-but-slightly-prejudiced ~~████~~) meaning

"The man who has no imagination has no wings."
                              — Muhammad Ali

My imagination is truly vivid and wild; I like to imagine what certain things feel like. For instance, having a knife thrust into my chest or my lung — the penetration of skin and flesh, the severance of nerves and tissue, like a needle poking through a thin bed sheet. The splintering of bone, then the slicing of an organ, then the extremely sharp pain that shoots through your system accompanied by blood seeping throughout your internal structure and flooding your organ. If it was your lung that was stabbed, it would fill with crimson essence, drowning you in a matter of minutes or seconds depending on the size of the blade. I guess I have given this too much thought or have seen way too many movies and real videos. I'm not saying I want to be stabbed... I just wonder what it would feel like. In cases like that or other misfortunate events I delve into the excruciating pain, I put myself into the mindset of the moment and when I feel it, my body becomes warm and adrenaline courses through me.

Same with having wings; I jump into the mindset of moving them, sending signals from my brain to my wings and I exert force to pump them up and down. Extensions of my scapula (shoulder blades) I feel them wings like they were regular appendages, it feels like the movement of arms flapping up and down... it feels natural.

When I imagine these situations, I believe it's happening. This emotional mindset helps my acting. Konstantin Stanislavsky a Russian actor, theatre director, teacher and co-founder of the famous Moscow Art Theatre, created a system that explains — or more respectively, educates one in the technique used to make an acted situation more believable.... the system is aptly named Stanislavsky Method Acting.

The Origin of the middle finger

The origin is speculative, but it is said that before the Battle of Agincourt in 1415, the French proposed to cut off the middle finger of all captured English soldiers, since the middle finger was used to pluck the English longbow. After the English won against the French, they yelled, "We can still pluck yew!" waving the middle finger.

Truth is, the infamous gesture can date way back, before the English and French... etymologists say the word "fuck" found its way into the English language during the 14th century, possibly from Dutch or Low German.

The middle finger gesture is much older, being referenced in a Greek play written back in 423 BC., "The Clouds." The gesture is also well-known to the Romans, so although the English "plucking" the French is a common theory, the actual origin is centuries older.

To all who hold grudges — don't waste your energy on something you possibly cannot or will not change! Live your life. If something happened with someone or a group of people just "be the better man and walk away." Believe it or not, it takes more guts to walk away from a conflict than to step up and do something (if it is a fight). If you walk away, you'll save yourself and the opposing party a bunch of time, and pain... although it feels good when my body is sore from a fight or training, but that's a different story. Masochistic much? Maybe... Back to the topic, I find great innocence in people eating. Even if it's a fat and disgusting slob pigging out, there is a level of innocence in people eating food. A family, little kids talking excited amongst one another with chunks in their mouths, a mother or father feeding a son or daughter, a boyfriend and girlfriend laughing during a meal together, an elderly couple.... no matter who they are, what kind of person they are, nobody should interfere with the appetite of others. I don't care if it's a low-life drug dealer, a murderous guerrilla militant, or person who stole money or a car from you—one should not strike another when eating. If the person happens to be a suspect from a crime, it's not a "last supper" kind-of-thing, it's just that I find a certain level of innocence in anybody and everybody when they indulge food.

What has this got to do with grudges? Isn't it obvious? Tis all just something you do not do (or should not do).

"The greatest wealth in life is the ability to learn."

"Genius is knowing to stay silent as others demonstrate their ignorance."

Albert Einstein — "Try not to become a man of success, but rather try to become a man of value."

"Confidence comes not from always being right but from not fearing to be wrong."

"When injustice becomes law, resistance becomes duty."

"If a law is unjust, a man is not only right to disobey it, he is obligated to do so." — Thomas Jefferson

"Choose a job you like and you will never have to work a day in your life."

"A champion is someone who gets up, even when they can't."

Have you ever thought of rhyming in another language? It's not like trying to rhyme in English because other languages don't exactly end words the same way English words do.

"You don't love a woman because she's beautiful, she is **beautiful** because you love her." — Although some may disagree, this is a very nice quote.

STAY AWAY FROM NITRATES!
They are preservatives that have been shown to increase the risk of cancer when consumed over a long period of time.

Jason Cameron, the television star and personal trainer, says getting good fitness results "is all about forcing the body to adapt to stimuli you're not used to."

When I look at cars as livings things and not as driven vehicles, it's kind of cute. When little cars make a 3-point turn or jeeps and SUVs speed in and out of traffic, they look like cute mechanical animals doing what they can to survive and going about their business. The larger automobiles are like elephants of the species, like trucks.

It is said humans are the worst balanced animals; how humans walk is described as a series of successive falls.

*   *   *

On a flight back to New York a few months ago, we were flying through a storm and watching the lightning crash through the clouds and inside them, at random spots in the sky, I was hit with the idea that this whole event looked like a battle of the gods! T'was fun to imagine it, my flight heading to NY at the same time a battle of the gods was transpiring — and we were flying right through. It was a sight to behold.

Experiencing it and knowing friends that go through it, I know all about families and their protective behavior towards their children, strict or not. Drama is annoying, stressful, and un-necessary, especially when it's within a family or at school, and it makes you feel frustrated or depressed when you can't do anything aboot it, or deal with it the right way, a way that won't be illegal and get you in serious legal action... unless the drama is so inhibiting that there's no other way than to deal with it in court.
Another pet peeve is family members talking behind each other's backs and smiling when in their presence. NOT NICE!

Memo: Isn't it annoying when a person curses WAY TOO MUCH? Where after almost every word is either "f*%.#" or "s*!#"... you have to be mindful of where you are (unless you <u>just</u> <u>don't</u> <u>care</u>), but I'm just stating in general how bother- some excessive cursing can be. If you were raised that way and have been around people that curse, then fine.... but there should be a level of self-control, especially when the time comes to be professional. Also, excessive cussing in a conversation can make the person sound uneducated. I do have to say, when you just don't want to hold in any more stress or animosity, cursing is a great way to get anger out.

RRRAAAA!!!

FACT
Did you know that the statue of Abraham Lincoln at the Lincoln Memorial was designed by a deaf man, and it's hands are posed in the sign language shapes for "A" and "L"?

The process of an experienced sign language interpreter signing away every word, every sentence is like watching a machine in an assembly line: speedy in its execution, precise and disciplined, every drop and rise, every sweep and motion as graceful as the next. With enough calibration and repair a machine is reliable. With enough training and practice a sign language interpreter is also reliable.
Both items are of high importance.

When I was a wee little lad, I thought words were pronounced exactly how they were spelled..., or at least how I perceived them to be pronounced. I was young and stupid (but cute to some of you), I didn't know any better. Words I thought were pronounced differently: elite = eh-leet. I thought it was eh-light.
Colonel = ker-null. I thought it was kuh-low-null.

In a relationship, when one spouse doesn't text or call for hours on end, and you have time to think... your mind wanders (or races) and your imagination runs wild. Even though you trust your lover, you start to worry.

The pressure of not knowing where they are or what they are doing, or if anything is wrong, is almost unbearable.

If you trust your friends, expect that they have their own agenda.

Heart-pounding   Tear-forming

Tension-building

Every day the body of an average person loses about half a quart of water just from breathing!

Hey!!! Guess what?! The head side of a penny weighs more than the tails side.

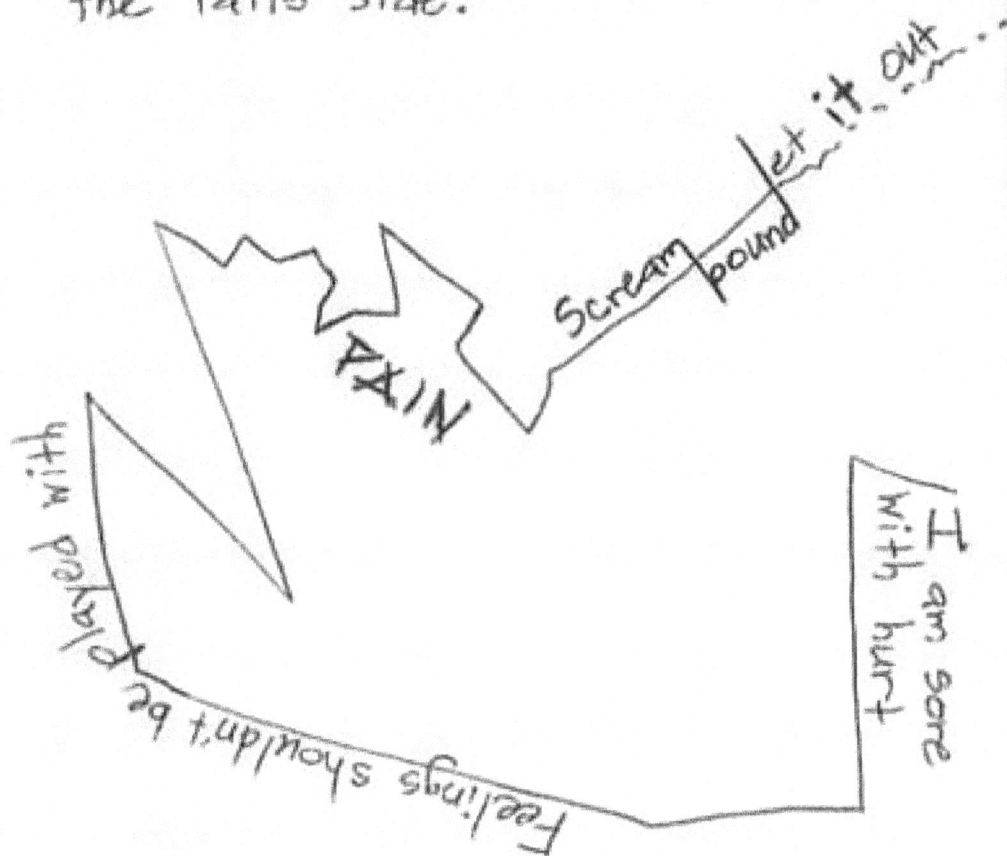

PAIN

Scream pound let it out...

played with

be t,uplnoys sbuilɘɘ⅃ (Feelings shouldn't be played with)

I am sore with hurt

I've been collecting damage... so apathetic... caught between two worlds, am I being hypocritical and not practicing what I preach by saying cherish a good relationship?

Everybody wants something to believe in, whether it's a higher power, a successful future or a positive outcome during a stressful situation. It gives us hope, a faith in good luck or a happy ending, so we can live better lives or at least look toward a better tomorrow.

— — —

Randomness is a fun thing. Entertaining to a mass selection of people and annoying to the rest.
Being random at times can help keep you sane in a world of schedules, time-is-money mentalities, and the stress of life and life's problems. Then there's the random happening of opportunities and chance.
Here in the Penn Plaza Border's book-store, I'm relaxing before meeting up with some friends back on long island, and I grabbed a few magazines (XBOX World 360, American Cinematographer, and Cineflex), and I picked an empty spot between bookshelves to read... and lo and behold, I spy with my little eyes a book by Leonard Mlodinow called

The Drunkard's Walk: How randomness rules our lives. How fitting the title is, to look up at a random book whilst taking a seat. I believe everything happens for a reason, seeing signs everywhere and the luck of meeting someone that can change my life or lead me in the right direction as a contact... or the chance happening of seeing a certain dvd or book that caught my attention, and after watching that dvd or reading that book, it helps me view life differently or it helps push me in the right direction, on my path to success. In today's world, 'tis challenging and difficult to have a good, happy life — especially since there are masses of stupid people that don't know how to drive, are cocky and arrogant, two-faced, niave/ignorant, and just pollute society by being on this earth.

Everyone deserves to live but there should be limits to allowing that. I'm not saying I'm God or that I should be judge, jury, and executioner...

What I'm saying is there are stupid people out there, people that have no common sense or open minds and if you happen to be one of those people you should take psychological and common logic tests, and if you fail, you should be transported to a certain living environment in another location with the rest of the people like you, and all those people should be looked after by the government. Then again, it would be like a bunch of egotistical, self-important wackos taking care of a group of idiots — it just doesn't work, the system cancels itself out. Hee hee.

The future's not for
me
in your
SOCIETY

[A <u>ribbon</u> round in a shotgun is a single-penetrating shell. A <u>buckshot</u> round leaves multiple holes in a target.]

Every year new structures and parks are being built. In the city there are more office buildings and condos being erected, but with the subways and buses getting more and more cluttered and with MORE cars on the road with MORE people driving each year, what will be done with public transportation and where will there be parking for the ones driving? And it is the 21st century, where are the skyscrapers actually scraping the sky, a metropolis of towers and buildings that stretch on for miles, and where are the flying cars and kick-arse hover boards? Or breakfast, lunch, and dinner in pill form? Or how about holographic tv and computer screens in every household? Ian and Chris (Loken) made a very good hypothesis: the human race has reached the pinnacle of its existence. Science and technology is advancing, especially with Japan continually creating new things, and new research (from any country) constantly uncovering formerly-unknown information, systems are upgrading, updating, and changing to become more sophisticated (like Switzerland's banks!), but it seems nothing great is happening in this lifetime aside from great research and record-breaking in sports.

Many can argue their point or opinion, but I have to agree with Chris and Ian... humans have reached a high and constant, unwavering point in their existence. It is stated given a long enough timeline, the life expectancy of everything drops to zero, and in history there have been extreme events of a species being totally wiped out, or at the very least become hit with a severe event that brings a species very close to extinction. Many have

said that humans are long overdue
in experiencing their armageddon
event. You only live once in this life,
I want to see something so incredible.

Convo w/ Samala, telling me
about ~~our~~ your attraction with
one another to sister Kitty

"Well we can't help it.." and she
was like "I know, believe me. You
two have this weird attraction
towards each other," and I was
like "Yes, that we do." haha.

When I'm with someone I truly love,
we transfer energies and I'm so
happy with the girl. Tis like we
both give off an aroma or some
type of pheromone that not only
attracts us to one another even
more but it's also that we give
each other a part of our hearts,
we sacrifice a part of our
bodies spiritually to one another
and all this makes the bond that

much stronger. I feel empty whenever I'm away from my significant other. When we're spending time together I'm so happy and complete, but when it's time to part ways 'til we see each other again, I get so down.... I get depressed because I want to be with that special someone who loves me and who gave a part of herself to me. It honestly feels like we complete each other...when we're so in love.

I don't care how old I get, I'm not growing out of having feelings for a certain someone. This human nature to love...to feel.

Aishiteru = "I love you"

Tada anata ga suki

I only love you   (Japanese)

I train my mind to make my body and actions assume a form that will accomplish my goals. I train my mind to make my body and actions assume a form that will accomplish my goals. I train my mind to make my body and actions assume a form that will accomplish my goals. I train my mind to make my body and actions assume a form that will accomplish my goals. I train my mind to make my body and actions assume a form that will accomplish my goals. I train my mind to make my body and actions assume a form that will accomplish my goals. I train my mind to make my body and actions assume a form that will accomplish my goals. I train my mind to make my body and actions assume a form that will accomplish my goals.

Make a mantra. Repeat it until it becomes second nature to recall. Allow it to be the drive in your life, or at least a part of the drive.

Is that the new 'thing' in Rap/Hip-Hop, or has it been going on for awhile? Performers in the genres are wearing sports hats of teams which logos are just the beginning letter that match the beginning letter of their names. For instance, this rapper named Plies uses the 'P' from the Pirates team logo and Chris Brown wears a hat from the Cubs team, which is just a simple 'C'. It <u>could</u> be their favorite team, but I'm not too sure that is the reason they're wearing them hats fer that reason...

——————————

There's a difference between being lazy and relaxing, and there's a difference 'tween procrastinating and taking your time. I keep certain responsibilities just so I don't get lazy...then again, being lazy isn't part of my nature, nor is it in my job description.

If I had it to give, I would

"Until we lose ourselves there is no
hope of finding ourselves."
— Henry Miller

"Human beings, who are almost unique in
having the ability to learn from the
experience of others, are also re-
markable for their apparent dis-
inclination to do so."
— Douglas Adams

You know that quote, "It's not like it's rocket science." Well, what if two rocket scientists were discussing how to successfully test-fire the Orion jettison motor to help further the development of Orion, NASA's Constellation Program's crew exploration vehicle... and one said to the other, "It's not like it's drug-dealing," or "It's not like it's a K'NEX set," something that rivals 'rocket science' in reverse? That'd be funny right? Right? I guess not.

★ Doctors giving viagra to babies? It is said to help relax constricted or tightened arteries in the lung of infants, and allows more blood flow to the lungs. If given too much, it can drop blood pressure. Also, it is stated there are no finished studies showing long-term effects of PRESCRIBING VIAGRA TO YOUR INFANT. Awesome. Hey— we found out this can help your sick baby, since Viagra does not have the same impact on children as it does on men, but as for RIGHT NOW, we don't know what it'll do to your child in the long run!!?

Have fun with that.

What's next, giving steroids to animals? I called it. Oh wait, that's already been done...crap. So much for that being my idea. *shrug*

Movies, to me, are more than just movies' now. Each movie has certain feelings to them, and I'm not justing talking about an emotion. I mean they have a certain color and shell. Then there's the movie that is based on a real event or real people, but movies are slowly starting to become reality; in The Day After Tomorrow, there were tornadoes in Los Angeles and more than 30 tornadoes have been recorded in Los Angeles County since 1918, but in December of 2004, a tornado struck the LA suburbs of Inglewood and Ladera Heights. Also, technology ▪▪▪ from films has been invented. What is seen onscreen is becoming real.

Another movie becoming reality: Minority Report. A University of Pennsylvania criminologist, Richard Berk, has been working with authorities to develop a software tool that predicts who will commit homicide. An article reads:

"The tool works by plugging 30 to 40 variables into a computerized checklist, which in turn produces a score associated with future lethality. "You can imagine the indicators that might incline someone toward violence: youth; having committed a serious crime at an early age; being a man rather than a woman, and so on. Each, by itself, probably isn't going to make a person pull the trigger. But put them all together and you've got a perfect storm of forces for violence," Berk said. Asked which, if any, indicators stood out as reliable predicators of homicide, Berk pointed to one in particular: youthful exposure to violence."

"The software is to enter clinical

trials next spring in ~~mostly in~~ the Philadelphia probation department. Its intent is to serve as a kind of triage: to let probation caseworkers concentrate most of their effort on the former offenders most likely to be most dangerous."

Besides the 'precrime' machine, the spider bots the PreCrime Unit use to search a house or apartment complex, is coming true: "BAE Systems just recieved $38 million from the US Army Research Lab to fund the Micro Autonomous Systems and Technology (MAST) consortium. The Point? To build an "autonomous, multi-functional collection of miniature intelligence-gathering robots that can operate in places too inaccessible or dangerous for humans."

http://www.druginducedcoma.com/2008/05/minority-report-is-coming-true.html >

Yet ANOTHER invention from Minority Report is the multi-touch screen. Jeff Han founded Perceptive Pixel, Inc. in 2006 and his aim is "to develop

and market the most advanced multi-
touch system in the world." I believe
Microsoft has copied the technology, if
not bought a patent or two, very
evident in the Microsoft Surface.

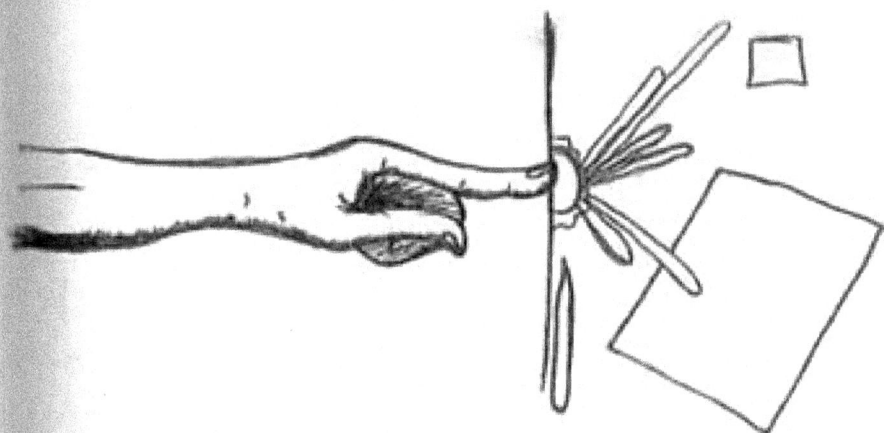

— My fortune cookie fortune:
   "You will be successful someday."
   Why tankoo!

— Another fortune: "The simplest answer
                   is to act."

... And another: "To affirm is to make firm

The world would be better if people
were that honorable, or disciplined;

the samurai never had to promise anything, what they said _was_ a promise. If a samurai were to say he would do something, it is as good as done. The warrior class lived a focused life, a willing death.

→ Big forearms, large upper body: ←‾‾
American intimidation.

In Union Square I met this gorgeous girl who has lived in Chile for awhile, and is now going to school here in New York. We started discussing love and people's bodies, and how ridiculous so many people are fake today, they live their lives by the media. This girl Julia said while down in Chile, guys would tell her she had big thighs and that she was thick. Those jackasses are thick... in the head. In manhattan, guys would walk by her and say out loud that they f*cked a girl that looked like her but thinner, and some others that would pass her told her she was too fat or had big thighs. What is WRONG with these idiots? I will tell you what's wrong with them: they're too infatuated with heroine-shooting - and - cocaine shorting anorexic whores who dress in skimpy attire then complain when being ~~wet~~ hit on and harrassed by all the wrong gentlemen. See, that was sarcastic; men who harrass girls and ladies are not gentlemen.

Anyway, all these blind and shallow morons insulting Julia cannot see true beauty. Superficiality at its most measured. They all took the blue pill and thus do not see the Matrix code, these bastards don't see people and things for what they truly are. Their definition of beauty comes in the surgery room and in pictures of vanity all over magazines, with botox syringes and liposuction hoses. Disgusting is it not? Their definition of hot and sexy is bony and TOO THIN with plastic implants that'll still be on your body after your flesh has rotted away in your grave.

The mentalities of these conformists is "pro forma," seeing things as a matter of form, not a matter of fact. Julia enjoys being comfortable, not only with her body but with what she wears. Agreeing with what she ~~always~~ asked, what happened to the voluptuousness of women's bodies?

The media monster is responsible for making women feel worried about their bodies, very self-conscious. And we're not talking about an issue of being healthy; this world is full of men and women that are not the average size that will live long lives. Men have been tuned in to eating healthy and losing weight and getting fit, but as for women, cosmetic surgery and accessories make the point of looking good gone too far.

Here's an article from Babble.com:

"According to a body survey in the UK mag Fabulous, women claim their ideal body size is a 6. When asked, men said they thought the ideal female body size should be a 10."

In UK measurements, a size 6 is a US size 4 and UK size 10 is a US size 8.

Skulls have become a symbol of pop culture. So have wings. And skulls WITH wings. They're everywhere: t-shirts, tv, album covers (although that's nothing new), and movies, among other faces of marketing.

"A dream come true is a tree of life."

+   o   +   o   +   o

"What's meant to be... will always find
              its   way"

It's really true to life... one example is
when I desperately want to find a song
and after hours and weeks of looking
for it online (inbetween my daily
schedule of course, I have a life ☺),
I kinda stop searching and I hear other
songs but I don't forget the one(s) I
really want. A few months to a year
later, I'll find the song on a friend's
computer or iPod, or I'll just happen
upon it. One song I struggled to find
with no avail, I finally found with no
effort on Amber's music player. "When
you are not looking for it, you find it."
Yes indeed.
Same goes for meeting certain people;
they either have connections that can
benefit you or you ▬ become lifelong

friends. If that person you meet never talks to you again, and you get somewhere because of their hook-ups, you at least have to appreciate them and be grateful for running into them. You have to be grateful and thank them graciously. People are in your life for a reason, a season, or a lifetime. Think back through your life, of all the people you've met or the things you were wanting and happened upon them later with little or no effort.

Put a goal out into the universe. Constantly think of that goal and believe you will reach it or acquire it, whether that goal is an item or a job or an ideal spouse. Allow that goal to become second nature in your thought process. The universe will know what you want and will help you get it after you write your goal down or think of it continually, but you cannot sit and wait to get it! You have to work towards it. 'Tis the law of attraction: the more you think of something—good or bad, positive or negative — you will attract it.

In 2007 I planned to get a new back-pack and new shoes. I didn't just WANT a new backpack and shoes, I PLANNED to get them. I BELIEVED I was going to get them, 'twas only a matter of time before I did. One week I stayed over Arnold's apartment, he gave me his old backpack while his roommate offered to give me a pair of new sneakers he didn't want. I was amazed! I didn't even relay the message I needed these items, they just asked me if I wanted to take them. See? The more you think of some-thing and the more you believe you will get it, the closer you will get to it. It works. "Thoughts become things."

It's been working in my life and the lives of many others, and I've been helping to make it work with my friends.

Knock, knock.

Who's there?

Alaska.

Alaska who?

Alaska round for directions.

13.7 Billion years ago, our universe used to be the size of an atom, smaller then the head of a pin... until one point in time there was a BIG BANG. Wow!

I see my life as a series of moments, and you probably do too. That's what life is, a succession of moments, good or bad. I see myself as people see me and I see myself as I see me. Think outside the box. I hear my thoughts and I repeat them to know what I thought, understand what I thought, what and how my mind is thinking. This is not a split personality trip, it's a critical thinking bit. My college class of Critial Thinking helped improve my on-purpose thinking.

"Whether you think you can or you can't, either way you are right."

—Henry Ford

The mind is powerful. If we are by ourselves and lack the discipline to motivate our bodies, it makes it difficult to accomplish a task. For example; if we're working out and don't set a goal of certain reps or we're running and don't set a certain distance to reach, we feel inclined to give up and not push ourselves to the limit, unlike when we are with another person or group of people which increases our motivation.

When we don't set a goal, our bodies tell us, "Okay this seems like a good time to stop," whereas when we do set a goal or we are with another, we feel like pushing a little further and our bodies say, "Let's do this. You don't give up on me and I won't give up on you."

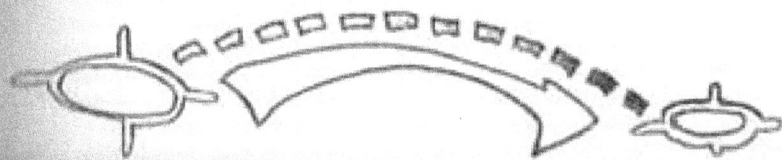

"The only way to discover the limits of the possible is to go beyond them into the impossible."

—Sir Arthur C. Clarke

This has had to happen to everyone at least once: you is walking down the street and someone is walking in your direction and you both try to walk one way but almost walk into each other. Upon realizing this you try and move to the left but that person moves that way, so you both move to the right, and it becomes this kind of dance.

Here's how to get past that: when that happens (when you two bump into each other, before "the dance"), stop and don't move until the person picks a side and continues on his or her way. That way you avoid making it look like you're trying to stop them from going on with their day.

Those that fall from the sky through Black rings, Are those of angels with No wings

LDL (low-density lipoproteins) cholesterol is bad cholesterol and HDL (high-density lipoproteins) cholesterol is the good cholesterol. A high level of LDL cholesterol in the blood is thought to be related to assorted pathogenic conditions. A high level of HDL cholesterol in the blood is thought to lower the risk of coronary artery disease.

Pathogenic: capable of causing disease

"Copy from one it's plagiarism. Copy from many, it's research."

US-CERT: United States Computer Emergency Readiness Team

That was a weird type of funny... when looking at the time and saying it in my head, instead of saying "9:30" for a split second my head told me "N:30"....but it's because the number nine starts with a "N" and that's how my head wrote it out before I corrected myself, haha.

Have you noticed when some shows go to commercials, the volume turns really loud, then when the show returns, the 'volume' gets low again?

"No I don't want to buy your crap or watch your stupid show. I understand you have to respect your sponsors by showing their commercials, but don't blast the sound when I'm trying to hear the voices of the people because your broadcast station decides to turn the show down so everyone in the household can hear commercials and be reminded of what they need or what they don't need but want..." * takes long breath * That was a mouthful.

SR71 is also a band name.

Mach 25 = 20,000 miles per hour. That's how fast the United States SR71 orbital fighter travels.

From reading and training, I can see the blood in my veins and my organs, see it rushing through my body. I can see the air enter my nostrils, into my lungs

and flow back out into the world,
   I see.... I feel... I feel every beat
of my heart, every click and gurgle of my
stomach. I feel blood flowing into my
muscles and soft electricity running to my
nerves every time I stretch in the morn.
I feel every tiny spazm of my skin, spazm
of a muscle, I feel every crack of my
bones stretching and twisting into movement...
I feel... I hear... I hear all the sounds of
my body, the beating of my heart.
Take all my senses and bring them out
into the world.... my senses of sight, smell,
hearing, touch, and tasting... and i have a
very acute sense of my environment. Being
grateful to be alive another day helps
increase those senses. ~~██████████~~
As for my conscious and psychological
perceptions, they change every few months;
when I see something or think of something,
my mind wanders on it and wonders about
every little detail, the what, the why, the
when, and the how. I analyze it. Then if
it's something I want to know more about,
know what's under the surface, I will delve

into learning more about it and then my perception of it changes. When I see that same thing years later, knowing what I know and thinking how I do, my perception of it changes yet again.

Take a movie for example: you watch it and after watching it, your memory of the movie stays with you (if you have a good memory, but many people remember pictures and something they SEE rather than something they READ, like words, letters, and numbers). Now watch that same movie 2, 3, or 4 years later. Depending on what you know now as opposed to what you knew when u first saw the film, your perception of it changes, no? It does for me, I'll either better understand it because of watching it many times over or because my understanding of life and people has changed. Give it a try sometime. You may see the movie differently.

You will always know more today than you did yesterday, and you will always know more tomorrow than today. –

"You learn something new everyday"

random. The word Manhattan means
fact : "hilly island" in the Native
American Delaware language.

The greatest power of the warrior
mind is its ability to act from Mushin, a
state of "no mind."

Sometimes the items that are really bad
for the brain have the best smell.
Gasoline, whiteboard markers, and paint.
Then there are everyday household items
that aren't bad like Snuggle fabric
softener, detergent, dishwashing liquid, and
Febreeze and Oust, among other things,
not including the conventional and
scented candles. And then there are wines
and items of hygiene like deoderants and
antiperspirants.

#

Talking about personal hygiene products,
when I was a kid, for a while Old Spice
sold a combo stick: antiperspirant that
was, at the same time, deoderant. Now, that
certain Old Spice stick is split in two,
one an antiperspirant stick and the
other a deoderant stick. Figured they

can make more money that way right?
Film distributors will do the same
tactic with DVDs. They'll package the
first 2 movies together but the 3rd by
itself, just with an extra disc. Why not
put the trilogy together? Not all
companies do that, thank goodness. I
just sounded real proper just now.

ƎNI⅃ⱯNƎᴚᗡⱯ
:ʎƃɹǝuǝ ǝɹnd ɟo ʇoɥs ⅼnɟɹǝʍod ʇsoɯ ǝɥꓕ

Stop me if you've heard this one—
   "Excuse me? Hi, can I ask you a quick
   question?"   You just did... tis
funny when people ask that.
As I emphasize my words in these pages,
and you read them, do you PRONOUNCE the
emphasis in your head or do you just
read the word AS A WORD, like you're
speed-reading? Unless you are speed-
reading and your thought process is so
fast that your head EMPHASIZES the
said words, while quickly taking in the
information you are reading... That is a
speedy head & eyes ya got there!

Art thou afraid of getting pricked by needles? Well, German researchers have discovered that coughing during an injection can lessen the pain of a needle stick. According to Taras Usichenko, author of a study on the phenomenon, the trick causes a sudden, temporary rise in pressure in the chest and spinal canal, inhibiting the pain-conducting structures of the spinal cord. **<u>NEAT</u>**▽
□

I was sick yesterday, but only for the better part of the day, I started feeling better in the evening. That's my record! The fastest my body took to heal used to be 3 days, now it is 1! I love the feeling of getting over a sickness, the energy and wanting to do things overwhelms me. Not only am I energetic, but I get such a <u>hunger</u>! Even when I do eat something while ill, I am still fiending for food. Like an ANIMAL hoarding the kitchen! DO RAWRR!
"Let us rise and be thankful, for if we didn't learn a lot today, at least we

learned a little, and if we didn't learn a little, at least we didn't get sick, and if we got sick, at least we didn't die; so, let us all be thankful."

— Buddha

"It is ironic for human beings to run faster when we have lost our way."

"Those who dance are often thought mad by those who cannot hear the music."

On the train, on the subway, at the airport, on the move... many different faces, many separate places. Have you ever, while driving on the freeway/parkway or while sitting in an airport, wondered where the person in front of you came from? Ever wonder where they are going? I'm not talking about stalking them, I mean visualizing a whole different thought process with a different set of emotions, picturing the smiling faces of their families or the warm embrace of their friends. I also visualize the places these strangers run to, the countries they visit... and it feels good to be somewhere else, traveling in that brief moment of a daydream.

Apex predator – A predator at the top of its food chain; a predator that is preyed upon by no organism.

Studies of the Human brain

Why you can't remember being born – You might think something as traumatic as birth would leave its mark on your memory, but chances are you'll only be able to remember back to age 5. One theory for this points to myelin, the protective nerve sheathing that helps with signal conduction; before age 5, a child's brain is low in myelin. "It may be important in long-term memory maintenance," states Jonathan Schooler, Ph.D, an assistant professor of psychology at the University of British Columbia.

Here's another possible explanation: As we learn to speak, we can no longer access memories created in our preverbal years. "With the onset of language, the way we think may change, making it impossible to 'get into the shoes' of our older memories," says Schooler.

Why you never forget how to ride a bike (unless you never learned) – When a child learns how to ride a bicycle, he (or she) makes 2 sets of memories: one is explicit memory, which records things like the color of the bike and the elation (joy, extreme happiness) of riding unassisted. The other set is implicit memory, which notes the body mechanics required to ride the bike, which is why it is sometimes called "muscle memory." Even when explicit memories fail, implicit ones remain.

Why you lose your keys – It's impossible (and impractical) to remember each detail of our daily lives, so our brains compensate by making memory generalizations called schemata (an underlying organizational pattern or structure; conceptual framework). For example, instead of remembering every apple you've ever eaten, your brain creates a schema of apples: hard, red, sweet. The same thing happens with your keys; rather than recall every instance of placing your keys on the dresser or desk, your mind creates a "keys = dresser" or "keys = desk" schema, so you have difficulty remembering the rare instances that don't fit the formula.

Finis

What is that I hear? If you're trying to make out what someone is mumbling at a party, lean in with your right ear? Why is that? It is because your right ear is better than your left at following the rapid rhythms of speech, according to researchers at the UCLA David Geffen School of Medicine. If, on the other hand, you're trying to identify that song playing in a café, turn your left ear toward the sound. The left ear is better at picking up music tones.

The old riddle, "Which came first, the chicken or the egg," is like asking which came first, the parent or the child? Tis a catch 22; there had to be one for the other to be.

An interesting picture book: <u>Wendal, His Cat, and the Progress of Man.</u>

*When we enter a new area, it's always a race. What it comes down to is the eternal balance in human nature — between what's in it for me and what's in it for us.

—SEED, a
science & culture
magazine

Have a nice _trip_, see you next <u>fall</u>
Don't stop moving forward, the
struggle is worth it in the end
once you reach what you want and
where you want to be in life.

EXIT ONLY
━━━━━━━━━━━━━━━━━━━

Don't take anyone's sh!t, do not
allow them to get away with their
deeds.

Remember, change in your life can
be beneficial; everything happens
for a reason!

"Those that take us back are
        memories.
Those that carry us forward are
        dreams."

Thy will be done.

www.ingramcontent.com/pod-product-compliance
Lightning Source LLC
Chambersburg PA
CBHW031833090426
42741CB00005B/226